HOW TO
BUY THE RIGHT
PLANTS, TOOLS &
GARDEN SUPPLIES

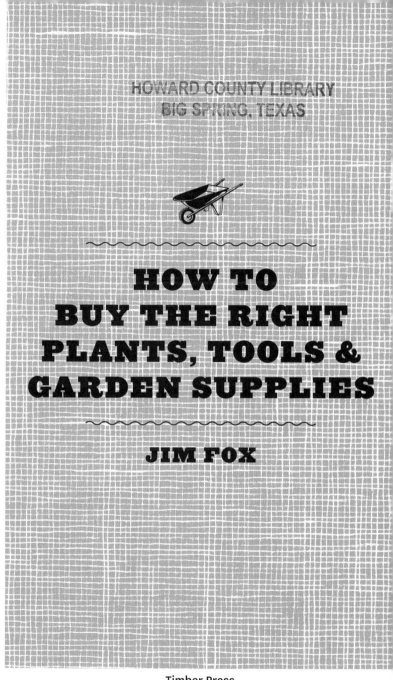

HOW TO
BUY THE RIGHT
PLANTS, TOOLS &
GARDEN SUPPLIES

JIM FOX

Timber Press
Portland · London

Published in 2013 by Timber Press, Inc.

Photographs by Marci Hunt LeBrun
Illustrations by Kate Francis

The Haseltine Building
133 S.W. Second Avenue, Suite 450
Portland, Oregon 97204-3527
timberpress.com

2 The Quadrant
135 Salusbury Road
London NW6 6RJ
timberpress.co.uk

Printed in the United States of America
Book design by Stewart A. Williams

Library of Congress
Cataloging-in-Publication Data

Fox, Jim, 1957-

How to buy the right plants, tools, and garden supplies/Jim Fox. —1st ed.
p. cm.
Includes index.
ISBN 978-1-60469-214-3
1. Gardening. 2. Plants, Ornamental. 3. Garden tools. I. Title.
SB450.97.F693 2013
635—dc23
2012027809

A catalog record for this book is available
from the British Library.

Contents

In memoriam: IJB, AS, LH, VE, GST, and Dean Long, who believed in— and expected—one's best.

Introduction

This book is a broad, practical overview of how to choose, buy, establish, and maintain plants and how to select wisely the implements and amendments that will help them grow well. It is based on my forty-plus years of experience as a keen student of gardening and horticulture; an avid collector of plants through nurseries, catalogs, exchanges, and botanizing in the wild; and a worker at various nurseries in customer service, as a manual laborer, as a buyer, and as a supervisor. In those forty years I have asked and been asked a lot of questions. I wrote this book to give answers to the most common questions, to explain horticultural jargon, and to give you the information you need to find and recognize quality plants, tools, and other garden necessities so you can spend your time and money wisely.

The first chapter will help you understand your garden's site and microclimates, learn about your area's climate and gardening zone, and ask yourself essential questions before buying your first plant or any more plants for your garden. You will learn to give thought to exactly what it is you want a plant to do for you—and to consider what your ambitions for your garden tell you about what to look for in a plant.

In chapter 2 you will learn where to buy—or not buy—plants. I show you how to evaluate a nursery, garden center, or mail order company, and what each offers that the other might not. I talk about what guarantees mean that come with a plant and what you should expect as a decent guarantee. Chapter 3 offers insight on how to read and decode the information on a plant label or in a catalog description. Chapter 4 gives basic information on the different types of plants—annuals, perennials, trees, shrubs, bulbs, and a host more—as well as what you should look for in a healthy plant.

In chapter 5 we move to considering how to select the garden tools that will be most useful to you and that will give you the best value for your money. We also consider the protective gear you will need to keep you healthy and happy as you work in your garden. Chapter 6 shows you how and when to put your investments in the ground and how to make sure they get off to a good start. Finally, in chapter 7 we look at the watering equipment, mulches, fertilizers, and pesticides you will need in order to maintain your garden, and how to water wisely.

Creating a garden can be a sizeable investment, and to the new gardener—and even the longtime gardener—buying plants and the supplies needed to nurture them can be daunting. Each year we are told of new, better, improved plants and techniques. Television shows and magazines encourage us to make our garden into another living space or a place to grow flowers for cutting and fresh vegetables for the table, or at least to make it into something that will improve the value of our homes. It is sometimes not clear if all this advice is helpful, hyperbole, or just another way to part us from our money.

I hope this book will help you make sense of the good advice along with the mystery, hyperbole, and overwrought mythology promulgated by friends, the media, and so-called experts when you begin choosing and buying plants, tools, and supplies. My goal is to educate you to be a savvy consumer so you can be confident that your gardening dollars are well spent.

1

What to Know Before You Buy

Walk into any nursery, pick out a plant you like, and the staff people will be happy to help you buy it. But is it the right plant for your garden? Do you know what the plant needs? Do you know what your climate zone provides in the way of heat, cold, and precipitation? Do you know what your soil is like—how it drains and how acid or alkaline it is? How much sun does your planting area get? What is it you want your garden to be or do for you—or more important, not be or do? How will you and your family (including pets) and service people use it? What do you already have in your yard? What's your budget? What are your abilities and ambitions?

If you want to make wise plant purchases, you need to know the answers to these basic questions before you venture out to the nursery. Nurseries are businesses. They, their catalogs, and their websites are set up to induce customers to fall in love at first sight with their many plants. I think we are just as hardwired to respond gushingly to a flower as we are to puppies, babies, sports cars, vacation spots, and granite countertops. But that doesn't mean the plant we fall in love with is the plant that will do well with what we or our yard can offer it.

Most of us know people who seemingly possess instant knowledge of what plant is right for any spot in any garden—the mystical green thumb. Whether consciously or not, these people have asked themselves the basic questions many times. Answering these questions provides a simple education about your likes and dislikes and about the land you plan to garden on. Without this knowledge, you're not gardening, you're making a stage set. You are decorating. That's fine. Nothing wrong with the latter, but that's another book you'll find in the theater section of your local or virtual bookstore.

It takes at least a year for anyone, novice gardener or expert, to really understand what will grow well on a new piece of property. If during that first year you are in a hurry to fill your yard with plants, buy annuals—plants that grow, bloom, and die in one year. Expenses are few, the lessons to be learned vast.

Your Climate Zone

"What zone is your garden in?" is typically among the first questions a nursery person will ask you—or you will ask yourself—when you're wondering about a plant you might want to buy. It certainly is an important question you must know the answer to each time you want to experiment with a new plant.

Climate zone maps have been created for most areas of the world, often based on average annual minimum winter

temperatures (and recently maximum summer temperatures), like the USDA plant hardiness zone map for North America (planthardiness.ars.usda.gov/PHZMWeb/), the hardiness
zone map for Europe (uk.gardenweb.com/forums/zones/
hze.html), and now the World Plant Hardiness Zone Map
(theplantencyclopedia.org/images/3/39/World_Plant_
Hardiness_Zone_Map.jpg). Today we understand that other
limits and needs also contribute to plant hardiness, including
length of growing season, summer heat, timing and amount
of precipitation, wind, and humidity. *Sunset* magazine has for
many years taken these conditions into account in its zone
maps, first created for the western states and now covering
all of the United States (sunset.com/garden/climate-zones/),
creating a much more accurate and valuable hardiness system. The Canadian government has similarly developed a
plant hardiness map for Canada that combines information
about a variety of climatic conditions (planthardiness.gc.ca/).

Learn your area's zone system and use it as a guide, not
the final word in hardiness. Every garden has its own varied
climate areas, some as simple as each side of the house, for
instance (see "Microclimates in Your Garden").

Most gardeners around the world find that their climate
falls into one of two categories: those where it freezes or
nearly freezes for long periods of time and all growth stops,
and those where freezing is nonexistent or rare and where
plants do or can grow year-round to some degree. In addition, there may be a rainy season along with a dry or drier
season to contend with. Much of the temperate world has
a mixed dry/rainy period during the growing season. In any
of these cases, depending on latitude there may also be
a long-daylight season and a short-daylight season—or
hours of daylight may be roughly equal in all seasons.

Microclimates in Your Garden

Microclimates, as the word says, are tiny climate areas in your garden different from the general climate zone of your neighborhood. Microclimates are influenced by a variety of factors, including orientation to the sun, slopes, prevailing winds, shelter created by buildings or plants, the soil, and the amount of moisture present in the soil. A microclimate can be an area where the sun is amplified by a stucco wall for most of the day, a bed where a gravel subsoil provides extra drainage and heat, a low area where cold settles, a place where water stands year-round, or a spot of shade provided by a big tree when in leaf. Such areas may be one or two climate zones warmer or colder than the rest of your garden.

You can discover your garden's microclimates by observing what happens over the course of a year. When many plants freeze to death in a severe winter, see if there is one of the same type that does not freeze in another part of the garden; if one does survive, you know that the area where it is planted is a warmer or more protected area for somewhat tender plants. Different microclimates can coexist within two or three feet of each other, providing all sorts of special areas for plants that otherwise might seem to be outside your zone. Find and exploit them.

Having a basic understanding of where your garden falls along these varied dimensions—freezing time, rainy and dry seasons, and light levels—will augment climate information to help you identify which plants will do better in your garden. For example, I grew up in Alaska where we had a frozen dormant season and a warmer growing season with yearly variable amounts of moisture in both. Nothing grew outdoors from October to late April. No exceptions. Nurseries did not sell plants for the outdoors in those months. The arctic influence and the diminishing hours of winter sunlight saw to that. Sometimes snowfall was minimal in the winter, causing the ground to freeze deeply and

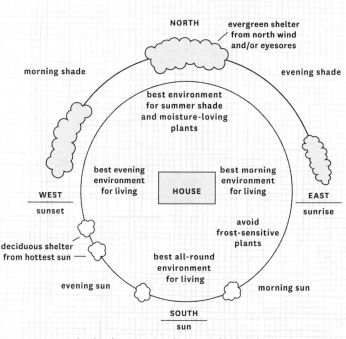

Every garden has its own microclimates, influenced by factors such as orientation to the sun, existing plants and structures, and prevailing winds. Observe and take advantage of yours.

plants to dehydrate. To prevent dehydration and have reliable snow cover, I would pile spruce boughs and twigs over some plants (the boughs and twigs allowed for air movement and moderated freezing and thawing). In the area of Alaska where I lived, natural moisture came at unpredictable times during the growing season and might amount to as little as sixteen inches of rainfall, resulting in semi-arid conditions during the growing season. Fortunately, the often cool summer temperatures prevented true drought. Warmer summers had me bringing out the hoses. When looking for plants for my garden, I chose those that could withstand cold, snowless winters; cool, mixed dry/rainy growing seasons; and summers with long day lengths and rapidly changing light levels near summer's end.

In Seattle, where I now live, it can freeze for short periods of time in winter when many plants are actively creating new growth, flowers, or roots. Redwoods rarely stop growing here except during a freeze that lasts for more than a day or two. Rain comes mostly in winter when light levels are low, humidity high, and fungal communities very active. So in Seattle I choose plants that can tolerate excessive winter moisture and potential summer drought, with longer daylight length during the drier summer season. I also know that I may have to use mulches to keep moisture in the ground or away from the crowns of plants to keep them from rotting during a warmish wet winter. Whereas in Alaska winter dehydration was my main worry for fully dormant plants, in Seattle my main concern is winter wet in a climate where many plants never truly go dormant.

In the jungles or junglelike areas of southern China, India, and the U.S. Gulf Coast, where there is no freeze (or rarely one), plants are on the job 24/7, year-round. There is usually a rainy or monsoon season, which may coincide with a long-daylight season, a short-daylight season, or days of equal length. Nurseries in these areas sell plants for the outdoors every day of the year, unless there is a season so rainy it makes it impossible to plant.

Moisture Levels and Soil Types

How well does your garden soil hold moisture? You'll want to know this when you're trying to decide whether a moisture-loving plant or one that needs good drainage is the one to take home. Soil moisture often has more to do with soil type than with levels of rainfall in your garden.

There are three major soil types: sand, loam, and clay. If your soil is sandy, watering it is like pouring water through a sieve or listening to a boring lecture: little is retained. A loamy soil, by contrast, has organic matter in it that acts like little sponges, holding and letting go of moisture as needed by the plants. A moistened handful, lightly squeezed, will hold its shape when you open your hand, something a sandy soil will not do. Press it with a finger and it will crack apart or break into two or three pieces. This is the soil most gardeners dream of. If you do the same trick with a clay soil, no matter how hard you press you will still have a clod of wet soil in your hand, one with a deep dent in it from your finger. Clay soil is made of tiny particles that bind together tightly, inhibiting water penetration or release.

There are beautiful plants for each of these soil types, but you must at least have some idea of which you have before you buy. You may have all three in even a small city plot. Most gardeners would find that a lucky gift. (See "Jar Testing for Soil Type" for an easy way to test your soil's type.)

To get an idea of the natural soil moisture levels in your yard, note where water lies longest in the wet season. Or where the existing plants go brown and die, or disappear beneath the ground until the next good rainy season. You might have lots of big trees shading the garden, sucking up all available moisture with their naturally greedy roots, making your garden droughty no matter how much rain falls. Take the time to observe these sorts of things before you buy.

Soil pH

Aside from your soil type, you should also have a rough idea of your soil's pH to be a wise gardener. The term **pH** refers to a measuring system to determine the acidity or alkalinity of your soil, which affects how well a plant can take up certain vital nutrients from the soil. The pH is rated on a scale from 0 to 14, with a soil pH of 0 being the extreme of acidity and a level of 14 being the extreme of alkalinity.

Most plants used in our gardens do well in soil with a pH ranging from 5 to 7.9. Many plants, however, such as rhododendrons, blueberries, and camellias, like more acid soils. Some alkaline-loving plants include pinks and carnations, lilacs, honeysuckle, and clematis. While you can modify the pH of your soil by using lime to "sweeten" it (move the pH to a higher number) or by using sulfur to make it more acidic (lower the number), it makes far more sense to choose plants that will do well in your soil at its existing pH. Personally, I prefer working with nature rather than fighting it.

To test the pH of your soil, you can buy a soil-testing kit at many nurseries or garden centers (or plant hydrangeas; see "Soil pH and Hydrangeas"). You mix a bit of soil from a

Jar Testing for Soil Type

A simple way to test your soil type requires nothing more than a large wide-mouthed jar and about a cup of garden soil (extracted from a hole you dig down into the root zone). If you think different parts of your yard may have different soil types, take a sample from each area. Remove roots and stones from the sample and put it into the jar. Then fill the jar almost full with clean water, add a few drops of dishwashing liquid, and put on a tight-fitting lid.

Next, shake the jar really well until you've broken up any lumps and clods so that they go into suspension. Leave the jar undisturbed to settle for two or three days and then check out the various layers that have settled out. The sand layer will have fallen to the bottom first, then the silt layer, then the clay layer. You can get a good idea of your soil type by noting the relative proportion of each type of particle in your soil.

couple of inches below the soil surface with the supplied solution and then stick a piece of supplied litmus paper in the solution. The paper turns a color that you then compare to the supplied chart that codes the colors to a specific pH level. You can also have a professional soil test done by a lab for a fee, which will tell you not only the pH of your soil but also the levels of various nutrients. It is a test well worth having done. The Master Gardener program, cooperative extension service, or national agricultural agency in your area may be able to suggest a lab to do this testing. Or go online to find one.

You should know if your soil is acidic, alkaline, or neutral, as many plants require one of these conditions. However, that said, you are less likely to have difficulties with alkaline-tolerant plants in acidic soils than the other way around. Thriving gardens full of alkaline-tolerant plants on the west side of the mountains in the Pacific Northwest—with its acidic

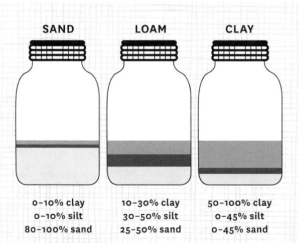

SAND	LOAM	CLAY
0–10% clay	10–30% clay	50–100% clay
0–10% silt	30–50% silt	0–45% silt
80–100% sand	25–50% sand	0–45% sand

Note the relative proportion of clay, silt, and sand in your soil to figure out your soil type. Sandy soil is 80 to 100 percent sand, clay soil is 50 to 100 percent clay, and loam is a relatively equal mixture of clay, silt, and sand.

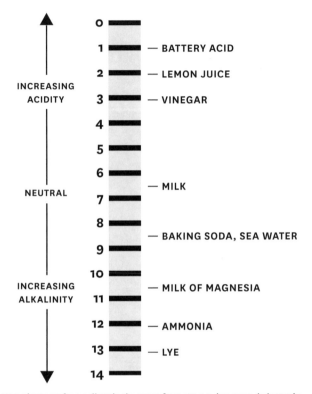

INCREASING
ACIDITY

NEUTRAL

INCREASING
ALKALINITY

0

1 — BATTERY ACID

2 — LEMON JUICE

3 — VINEGAR

4

5

6

— MILK

7

8

— BAKING SODA, SEA WATER

9

10

— MILK OF MAGNESIA

11

12 — AMMONIA

13 — LYE

14

Most plants prefer a soil pH in the range from 5 to 7.9, but some do better in acid soil and others in alkaline soil. Choose plants that do well in the range your soil offers.

soils—prove the point. Gardens full of acid-loving plants like rhododendrons, camellias, and gardenias are seldom found on chalky soils or the alkaline desert soils in the American Southwest—and not because of the heat and drought the latter has. However, since lime from limey subsoils does not travel upward, a deep layer of acidic topsoil over such areas will retain some acids until leached out by the rain.

Soil pH and Hydrangeas

One way to tell the pH of your soil is to plant hydrangeas—particularly those called mopheads or lacecaps. Alkaline or "sweet" soils make some of these hydrangeas bloom pink. Acidic soils turn the blossoms blue. This is why you buy a blue hydrangea, plant it by a concrete patio, and notice a couple of years later that the blooms are pink, no longer blue. Concrete has lots of lime in it, making the soil sweet.

Not all hydrangeas are so mutable; some cultivars remain a stable color. But if a cultivar is changeable, you can use lime or potassium sulfate to push it to pink. Sulfur, derived from aluminum sulfate, turns it blue. The change does not happen immediately but takes a couple of years to occur. Do not try to hurry the process by dumping loads of either product on the soil. You can poison the soil and the plant with too much of either. If your hydrangea is planted near a lot of concrete, get used to it being pink.

When you buy a hydrangea with a blossom described on the tag as blue but the flower is pink, this means the grower used water with a high lime content. If your soil is naturally acidic, the color should turn to blue in time.

Sun and Shade

Where does your garden get full sun, where is it in full shade, and where does it receive part sun, part shade, or dappled light? This is something you must make a point of observing during different seasons before you can know what will grow well in the space you have.

Full sun and full shade are opposites. The first refers to sunlight shining on an area all day long. Full shade is when sunlight is blocked from shining on an area all day. This may seem obvious, but understanding these definitions is often complicated because of when you work in the garden. If you always work in the early evening and the area is always sunny then, you'll be inclined to think, "Oh, it's a

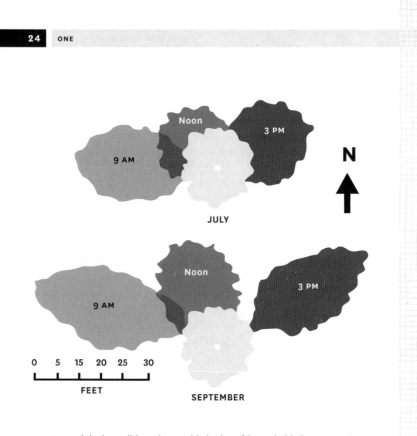

Sun and shade conditions change with the time of day and with the seasons. A 20-foot tree casts a different shadow in July and in September.

sunny area," not recalling or fully grasping that it's a shady area in the morning or at noon. If a plant evolved in hot sunny areas, it will love the sun at its most powerful, needing massive doses of sunlight to run its chlorophyll factory. In shade it simply has less power to grow properly, to resist diseases, and to withstand the vicissitudes of winter.

Part sun and part shade mean the same thing. Some part of the day there is one or the other. A plant labeled as liking one will like the other, though some plants will need cool sun or will tolerate hot sun. Morning sun is cooler. When the sun is lower on the horizon, it doesn't warm the air as quickly as it does when beating down from overhead later in the day. The sun's rays are very powerful just before, during, and after its daily zenith, which is midday.

To understand dappled light, think of a sieve or netting. Dappled light is tiny bits of light and shade falling on an area at the same time, most often caused by leaves on the branches of trees forming tiny moving gaps open to the sky that allow sunlight in. Because the gaps are ever moving, no one spot has long exposure to the power of the sun's hot rays. Dappled shade will give enough hours of sun for you and me to produce vitamin D and remain healthy but not enough to cause sunburn. If a plant evolved in the dappled light of woodlands or a cooler climate, that's what it will need. In hot sun it will transpire moisture faster than it can

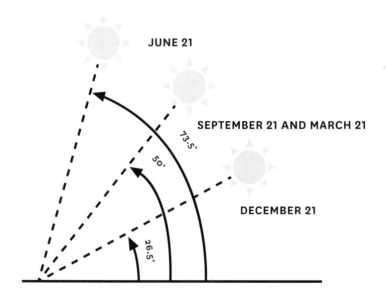

Observe your garden for an entire year to see the effect of the sun being low in winter and high in summer.

pull it up from the ground and will toast, its cooling and feeding system exhausted. Think how much better you do on a hot summer day sitting under a pergola covered with vines than in direct sun, sweating and overheating.

It's important to remember that shade and sun conditions change with the seasons—another good reason to get to know your garden through an entire year. The sun is low in winter and high in summer and thus able to reach over tall buildings and trees. Trees that drop their leaves during winter suddenly expose the ground beneath to light, albeit a cooler light. Evergreen trees usually hog the light year-round except during the shortest days of winter, when a sun low on the horizon can reach under the branches of many a tree; thus, you will need a shade-tolerant plant beneath.

Houses, fences, and neighbors' perpetually parked RVs also provide consistent shade. If you live in an urban area, sometimes an office building clad in glass will reflect intense light into a shady corner of your garden for a brief moment, illuminating it like some solstice shrine. It is important to know if such a Stonehenge effect happens in your garden. In five minutes this magnified light can burn a plant otherwise in shade for most of the year. It happened in a garden I once had.

If you have a sunny, moist area in your garden, think of all the plants that grow alongside sunny lakes or streams—primroses, astilbes, rodgersia, and the magnificent gunnera, which looks like a gigantic, prickly prehistoric rhubarb. These plants will grow lushly with their roots in cool, moist soils, while their leaves revel and their flower colors dazzle in the sun.

In drier woodland conditions, it is the many spring ephemerals that give us hope and joy at winter's end or spring's beginning: think of anemones, snowdrops, trilliums, lilies of the valley, ferns, and Solomon's seals, to name but a few. Others, protected by the canopy of leaves, remain evergreen during the summer, providing texture and variations on the theme of green, and then produce colorful fruits and leaf tones in autumn.

Your Garden's Purpose

Every garden should have a purpose, and the earlier you understand this purpose in the planning stages before anything is planted or removed, the more satisfying your garden will be. What do you want your plants to do? This is a *very* important question. Plants, like most events and things in our lives and homes, can serve a purpose or can be potential problems we should try to anticipate. Plants can provide protection, direction, comfort, beauty, food, habitat for birds and bugs, memories of friends and places past. They can also get in the way; cause damage to roofs, driveways,

Community Rules and Regulations on Trees

If you live in a city or subdivision with ordinances on tree height or other restrictions on the cutting down of trees, you'd better check these ordinances and understand them. Some communities have absurd laws about cutting down trees that reward people who leave huge trees susceptible to wind damage or to falling on your or your neighbor's home, or on the street. Well intentioned as these regulations may be, in the name of keeping our neighborhoods green, they take little account of how such big trees behave in urban landscapes where their roots are constantly cut by cable and electrical companies, sewer and water utilities, and house expansions, or where they are restricted by sidewalks, roads, and foundations. Regardless of the logic, or lack of it, you do not want to run afoul of these local regulations.

sidewalks, and water and sewer systems; or end up losing their charm and value for any number of reasons—not unlike friends, homes, or partners we outgrow over the years.

I always tell myself that a plant, like me, has a job to do in the garden. It has to pull its own weight as part of the home and household. Here are some questions to ask yourself about each plant you have or want:

» What is the plant's job? Why is it here?
» Is it worth having around anymore?
» Does it have such great sentimental value that I will do anything and everything to help or save it?

Answers to these questions can be as varied as gardeners themselves are, but usually answers about a plant's job can be placed in these simple categories:

» This plant is to impress people and the community at large with my horticultural prowess or large bank account.
» This plant is to help me surround myself with beauty while at home.
» This plant hides something from my gaze—such as neighbors' houses, an ugly building, a utility station, an unpleasant view, or the mess my kids make in their part of the garden.
» The plant gives me a place to indulge my hobby and myself.
» The plant delineates an area for play, quiet, exercise, or entertaining in my yard. (Today this is marketed as "outdoor living," as if one can be outdoors and not live.)
» The plant provides food to enhance meals and lower food expenditures, or flowers for indoor decoration.

» The plant provides shade during the summer or blocks prevailing winds during the winter.

On the other hand, here are a couple of potential answers to the question of whether a plant is worth having around anymore:

» The overgrown hedge needs to be removed because it is ugly and a rat haven.
» The large maple, while lovely, majestic, and useful for providing shade, is damaging the foundation of the house, cracking the sidewalks, and invading the sewer line.

There are hundreds more reasons each of us can think of for putting plants in or taking them out. Where you decide to put plants in or take them out will be influenced by your consideration of these items as well:

» The views you want to have or to save from both inside and outside of your house. Do you need your children's outdoor play area to be visible from inside the house so you can easily monitor them?
» Where your sewer, water, and other utility lines are— below or above the ground.
» The best access to parts of the garden and house. You don't want to block off firemen from a part of the house or force the people bringing in your grand piano to crush some prized plant that you greedily put too close to a walk.
» Where you want the private and the public areas of your yard and garden to be. You don't want to scare the neighbors while you sunbathe. On the other hand, you might want your neighbors to feel free to join your outdoor barbecues, so this area should be where they can see it and feel free to enter.

The more time you give to critical thinking about your garden, the better it will suit you and the plants you put in it. I suggest you take a year. Live through each of the seasons. Get to know where the patches of sun and shade are, in which season. Discover where neighbors use their yard, keep their pets, park their cars. Learn where salted snow is piled by the street plows or where the deer like to browse.

If you are completely flummoxed as you consider your garden's purpose, bring in a garden or landscape designer for an hour or two of consultation. He or she can see more in one hour than you could in six months. Be honest with the consultant about what you want and do not want. Expect honesty in return. Blunt questions or answers are not rudeness in this instance. Remember, you are paying for expertise by the hour. It's better to get an honest if painful critique of your garden than a wishy-washy one that leaves you with no firm ground to stand or plant on.

Your Preliminary Plant List

Now that you are armed with information about your garden's purpose and current conditions, it's time to figure out which plants can grow in those conditions that also fit your needs and desires. It is important at this point to realize and accept that some plants you believe you must have will not actually grow on your property. Either come to terms with this or call your real estate agent. Not only can you not fool Mother Nature, it's tiring to fight her every day or each winter—unless you're an eternal optimist with little long-term memory of disappointment, or a horticultural masochist.

Begin your plant list by taking a walk around your neighborhood. Stroll around on a spring morning or summer's eve and notice who has beautiful gardens and what plants are growing there. If you see sprinklers running and water sheeting off the sidewalk or driveway, this tells you that that lovely garden may be a bit of a cheat. Other gardens will look lush and overgrown with no sign of watering. This is where you should take notice. What do you see growing there? Also note which ground covers are used and if they've invaded lawns or sidewalk cracks, or gone under the fence into the neighbor's garden. These are plants to be leery of. Are there vines swamping big trees, choking others to death, or politely reclining on roofs, sheds, or neighboring plants?

Homes and gardens that have been abandoned show which plants thrive on neglect in your climate. Ask yourself if these plants are beautiful and behaved, or thuggish. Are there some that are barely surviving? All important clues to what will do well for you.

After a record cold or hot spell, go around and note which plants survived well. Note their position in relationship to sun and shade. Does that big tree two houses down look like it was planted decades ago, or recently after a remodel? Do you find combinations that look good together or make you gasp in horror? Have the plants persisted year-round in mild climates, or in colder climates do they appear from the melting snow just as they looked when the first snow fell? If a plant is doing well, notice if it's in shade year-round, or in sun, or in a wet seep. Have children, dogs, or volley-ball games harmed the plants or have the plants enjoyed the company? Do most lawns go brown at the same time or remain green with little or no apparent irrigation? Take photos, sketch plants, or ask someone out in that yard or in the neighboring yard if they know the names of any of these plants you're looking at.

Then get out and visit local public gardens to see which plants can be expected to grow in your area. Many public and botanical gardens grow plants on a trial basis to learn which do best in an area or what they require to survive well in your area (see "Plant Evaluation Programs"). All public and botanical gardens are, in a sense, test gardens. Many nurseries and garden centers have display plantings of some sort that always have something to teach you. Always have a notebook and pencil on hand when visiting gardens. Soon you will have many notes and free lists of plants to choose from for your garden. More, in fact, than you could ever find room to plant and grow well.

Your Budget

Now give some thought to your budget. Money doesn't grow on trees, but trees and other plants do cost money, even if you grow your own. Even trading involves an initial investment in a plant that someone will want in trade from you for something they have. Gardeners are a grand and generous fraternity, yet some plants must still be purchased.

A new garden, from bare earth to finished beauty—which includes plants, hardscapes (patios, walkways, retaining walls), and any wooden structures or outdoor cooking areas, plus the labor to install them—usually costs 10 percent of the purchase price or assessed value of your home. You can spend more or less, all at once or over a long period of time, but this is a rough rule of thumb.

Figure out right away how much you can afford to spend each year before you go to the nursery to purchase your first plant. You also need to have some idea of what figure you are going to exceed, or negotiate with your partner, spouse, or bank. (One should never have to negotiate with one's self. It only leads to therapy, and that money is better spent in the garden, which provides excellent mental and physical therapy whether you are sitting or working in it. I speak from decades of personal experience.)

Your Abilities and Ambitions

As you contemplate your plant list and garden plans, you must be absolutely honest about four crucial points:

» how much time you want to—or can—put into working in and maintaining your garden
» what your horticultural skills are—or aren't
» whether you can afford to or want to have someone else come in to do the work
» how much you are willing to pay for water each month

A lovely large garden can be created that takes no more than an hour or two a week to maintain, along with a couple of half to full days in autumn or spring to clean up or replant. I know—I've done it. The great English gardener Graham Stuart Thomas reckoned his three-quarter-acre garden took less than fifteen six-to-eight-hour days per year to maintain. However, another great English gardener, Christopher Lloyd, believed that if you aren't working in your garden daily you aren't gardening. To each his own.

Myself, I don't believe gardening is a contact sport. I strive to give plants the conditions they want and then leave them alone, occasionally coming in to rip out a thug or coddle a plant of great sentimental value unless I decide it is just too needy for me, so out it goes. I will redo a planting if needed because of weeds or poor design or lack of visual interest, but to garden daily—that's not for me. Horticulture is but

Plant Evaluation Programs

Listed here are just a few of the most prominent plant evaluation programs. Many states, provinces, and countries conduct similar trials.

In the Pacific Northwest, the Great Plant Picks program seeks to evaluate and recommend a broad range of plants that do well primarily in the Puget Sound area (though the committee strives to cover an area from Vancouver, British Columbia, to Portland, Oregon). The plants must do well in the region, have a history of being easy to grow, provide good value, and be readily available.

The Pennsylvania Horticultural Society (PHS) operates the Gold Medal Plant Award program for "trees, shrubs and woody vines of outstanding merit." The plants are evaluated and chosen for their year-round visual appeal, performance, and hardiness in USDA zones 5–7. They are also selected for pest and disease resistance, and are easy to grow with PHS's recommended techniques.

one of several things I live for, and there are so many gardens and gardeners yet to visit.

Whether you want to have the biggest collection of rhododendrons or maples or cactus or dahlias in your area, be honest about what will be required, what you are capable of doing, and what you will put up with in the way of the "natural" look.

Your Final Plant List

You're almost there. It's time to go through that list of plants you've made to weed out those you now know won't thrive in your garden and to expand on those that fit your

The Chicago Botanic Garden has plant evaluation gardens for sun and shade where thousands of plants are evaluated over several years for hardiness, performance, and beauty. The botanic garden's very useful reports on specific genera, available online, are issued on a semi-regular basis.

The JC Raulston Arboretum in Raleigh, North Carolina, is constantly evaluating and reporting on plants that perform well in southeastern U.S. gardens and possess merit and beauty.

In the United Kingdom, the Royal Horticultural Society has been operating the Award of Garden Merit (AGM) program for nearly a century. It looks for plants that do well in U.K. climates, provide good value, and are true to their description, going so far as to evaluate plants sold by various nurseries to see which are correctly named and which have become muddled in the trade. Reports from the trials are issued online now, but paper copies can also be obtained.

site, budget, and ambitions. Mark the sun lovers for your shade-free yard or those that can be pruned into hedges and parterres for your faux French cottage. Remind yourself that you can always add more plants later. This part of gardening—editing—is the greatest and hardest part of the art—of any art!

Once you've vetted your list like a horticultural Santa Claus, you are ready to go looking for the plants, indulging in that great capitalistic pastime—shopping.

2

Where to Buy Plants

Now that you know what you can grow and what you want, where do you find plants? The options in this Internet age are many: local garden centers, nurseries, garden store chains, garden centers attached to big box stores, local plant sales, neighbors, plant society exchanges, and mail order. A basic goal for you is to find a good, honest supplier—one you can trust and build a relationship with. This chapter will give you the background to do that.

Nurseries and Garden Centers

There's nothing like walking around a retail garden establishment in the springtime to get the creative juices flowing. You can choose from among nurseries (which can be small family-run businesses or large-scale operations), garden centers, and big—nonnursery—box stores. What, you may rightly ask, are the similarities and differences among them? After all, they all sell plants. The answer is simple:

all but the big-box stores are primarily in the business of horticulture.

Still, you can find great plants at good value at all three places, and you will find substandard plants, too. All these businesses deal with a live product. You shouldn't expect perfection every day. But you should always expect the plants to look healthy and vigorous, be properly named with a common and a botanical name, and be informatively labeled or described in an available catalog; the public area

Nursery, Garden Center, and Garden Visiting Etiquette

» Do come with questions. There are no stupid questions.
» Take notes. Come with paper and pen, or your electronic note-pad, to note what you see and what you are told.
» Don't remove tags or labels in place of taking notes.
» Keep to the paths in gardens and to the sales area in nurseries. Don't go into backstock areas or mill around trucks unloading plants, if only for your own safety.
» Leave your pets at home unless it's specifically noted they are allowed, but then always on a leash for their protection and safety from parking lot traffic, milling feet at the counter, and other animals less well behaved than yours, as well as in deference to local leash laws and out of courtesy to the owner's own pets on site.
» Teach children to be respectful of the plants and customers, for their own education and the safety of others.
» Put plants back where you found them or ask a staff person to help do that.
» Walk around, read labels, and soak in what's on offer.
» Don't feel any pressure to buy.
» Feel free to shop away.
» Remember that we all have good days and bad days. It's nothing personal.
» A smile works every time.

should be neat and tidy, and there should be an informed and helpful—but not hovering—staff.

Nurseries

Nurseries are the places that should, by definition, sell plants they grow or that they buy in as small plants and "gown on," to use industry jargon, to a larger, salable size. But in the United States, the word **nursery** is as often applied to a garden center type of business where only a few of the plants for sale were grown by the business and there may be a few accessories for sale besides. In either instance, the focus is on the plants, and staff members know the plants intimately. A large nursery will have plants for sale as the seasons permit and may close during the off season or may sell plants year-round. Many have display gardens to show how particular plants grow, to showcase and test plants new to the market, or simply to inspire and entertain customers.

Nurseries can be big operations, small family enterprises, or a collector's way to cover the cost of a hobby gone wild. Whichever, all exist to sell plants. The people there live and breathe horticulture. It's a passion and a business.

Garden centers

Garden centers may grow some of their own plants and may even attach "nursery" to their name, especially in the United States. But generally if you walk into a place noted for selling plants and see tools, books, candles, sculpture, clothing, holiday decorations, and coffee and pastries for sale, along with lots of plants in pots brazenly labeled with a commercial grower's name, you are at a garden center—a one-stop shopping spot for all your gardening needs.

Garden centers also differ from nurseries in always having big sales at the beginning or end of the growing season—a standard business practice meant to get you in to spend money, or to reduce the inventory of plants as the business's prime focus turns toward holiday gifts and other nonplant purchases. There are plant-passionate people at garden centers, too, some of whom when given the chance create beautiful and inspiring container plantings or display gardens.

Big-box stores

Many large building supply, grocery, or hardware stores have garden centers attached to them. In the United States, they are usually seasonal; in the United Kingdom, they can be there year-round. It's important to remember that for these big-box-type and chain stores, selling plants is a very small part of their business. In many of these stores in the United States, the plants are sold at a loss in order to draw customers in.

Early in my career I worked at this type of store; though I wasn't in the garden center, I saw what happened to the plants and learned what the store's position was. The plants are enticements to get you in to buy fertilizer, tools, soil, bricks, pesticides, lumber, and other hardware. The plants are so limited in value to such businesses that, more often than not, the wholesale nurseries that sell the plants to them are not paid for their plants until the store sells them to you. If the plants die while in the care of the big-box store, it loses nothing—the grower does. (Recently some small commercial growers have begun to offer similar "returnable" plants to small nurseries and garden centers. They are purchased by the nursery but with the clause that if it has not sold, the plant may be returned to the grower for credit *only if still alive*. This is a good trend.)

You should ask yourself: If the big-box store is not willing to purchase the plant, why should you be? The cliche "You get what you pay for" was invented with such businesses in mind. What seems like a great price is so only if you buy the plant within 24 to 48 hours of its arrival at the store. Stores have different delivery days, so if you choose to patronize such places, find out when deliveries are made and shop within a day of that delivery.

Be wary of diseases at such places. Tomato- and potato-blight outbreaks in the United States have been directly linked to certain such stores by reports in the national press in recent years; heirloom tomatoes are particularly susceptible to infection and hosting of these blights. (Though in fairness, the rise in interest in heirloom tomatoes has caused blight to spread throughout all garden businesses.) Buy with caution.

Sales: True Value or Not?

At any of the kinds of retail establishments just described, be cautious when shopping during a sale. Excellent bargains are to be had, certainly, but to know whether you are really getting a bargain, there are many things you need to understand.

Some sales feature true savings that a nursery or garden center passes along to customers from its supplier. When nurseries in areas of severe winters need to sell off their outdoor plants, unable to keep them in good condition over the winter, those sales are also often full of good values. And bargains can be found when stores reduce prices simply because they need to boost sales at a certain time of year or reduce overstocks of a particular item that didn't sell as well as hoped. The sales that require you to be cautious and careful are sales meant to rid a business quickly of plants past their prime, to free up the space they occupy for the next season's plants or other merchandise, or to lull you into thinking you are getting a bargain; this is especially true with the most seasonal of plants—annuals and vegetables.

The first thing to bear in mind when shopping a sale is what were the prices of the items during the regular season. Some businesses bring in plants or other items, raise the price, then have the sale. For example, note what a maple tree's normal price is in spring and summer. The tree may sell out at this price by late summer. In autumn when the maple takes on vibrant autumnal coloring, the nursery will buy more of the same size at the same price as the earlier one but initially price the tree higher than it was priced in spring, so that when it's offered on sale at 20 percent off, the savings simply means that you pay a slightly lower or even a slightly higher price than the spring and summer price. While this is not a common practice, it does happen too often, so it's important to pay attention to plant prices during the regular sales season.

Spring and autumn sales are often created to get you into the nursery to buy plants and sundries other than those on sale, a practice common in many businesses. If you know the prices and quality of plants at your local plant stores most of the year, you may find good deals at sales, but don't do your shopping just because you see a "Sale" sign, thinking you are getting a deal. Too often you may not be.

Guarantees

A true guarantee offered by a nursery or garden center must reflect the responsibilities of both parties—the business and the buyer. Plants are living things. They can be injured or mistreated by either party, by mistake or by deliberate actions. A plant seller is responsible to sell you a healthy plant, labeled correctly, and to answer your questions on care of the plant accurately, given the information you provide. Once you take possession of a plant, its health and care become your responsibilities until it becomes established—and beyond. It is your responsibility to ask how to care for it if you do not know how to do so. It is also your responsibility to follow any instructions given, and to accept the results if you don't (provided the instructions were correct).

If a plant does not perform as expected or dies, go back to the company that sold you the plant and question why it is not thriving or why it died. Ask "Did I do something wrong?" in order to possibly learn something new or discover you did nothing wrong. Mistakes can be made on either side of this transaction. A third party could have harmed your plant. In any case, a good nursery will always work with you to learn why the plant is not doing well or died, and to make good any mistakes made while the plant was in the care of the nursery or its supplier.

It is important to understand that both parties in this partnership are at the mercy of Mother Nature or "acts of God." If it is clearly indicated on the label that a plant will not survive your garden's conditions—cannas will not be perennial in Alaskan gardens nor will cold-loving plants do well in tropical areas—do not expect a replacement. Nor can a nursery or garden center **ever** be responsible for the results of unusual weather conditions. However, an incorrectly written label or mistaken employee can and should be held responsible.

Many businesses offer a one-year, no-questions-asked guarantee on their plants. Sounds good, doesn't it? It's not. In reality, it's a pretty worthless guarantee when it comes to plants. A plant that takes a year to die nearly always has suffered while in your care—perhaps not by your hands but rarely if ever from something the seller did since those injuries show up fairly quickly at the nursery. And "no questions asked"—isn't that a sticking-your-head-in-the-sand attitude? Don't you want to know why your plant did not succeed? I do. Was it my fault, my neighbor's, a family member's, the cat's, or the nursery's? Such guarantees cannot even be called a guarantee. They are simply a technique to get you back into the store to spend more money on other items. Such guarantees always make me suspicious. I want to learn how to grow the plant. I do not want to be placated, patronized, and sent on my way, perhaps with poor information and another plant soon to die too.

The best "no questions asked" guarantee states that plants are healthy, correctly named, and properly labeled as to their needs and growing conditions. It also states that you may return the plant in thirty days, no questions asked, for a full refund as long as the plant is in salable condition in its original container and you have proof of purchase— the original tag or a store receipt. (Usually once a plant has been removed from its pot and planted, a nursery cannot sell it again because of possible contamination from pathogens in the soil. This is horticulture's version of the garment industry's no-return policy for worn swimsuits.) The guarantee should also say that if a plant looks ill or has died after being planted, you can bring it in or come in to discuss possible reasons, where responsibility lies, and what cures or financial compensations are available.

Think of buying plants as a business transaction that is really a partnership, best maintained with open communication, honesty, and a good dose of forgiveness from both parties, not unlike a marriage. As soon as a plant dies or does not look well, contact the seller. A reputable nursery will help you figure out the problem and do right by you if the problem originated with them, oftentimes going beyond its legal or moral responsibilities, especially if you arrive with reasonable expectations.

All gardeners make mistakes—even you. And even me.

In my experience, the top two killers of plants are improper watering and improper siting (which includes burying the root-ball too deeply). Most gardeners cannot believe they would ever do either of these things. But they do. I have done it and still do on occasion, I confess. The late Steve Doonan, a horticulturalist who was internationally famous for his ability to grow almost any plant, would tell all gardeners: "Remember, great gardeners are great gardeners because they have the biggest compost piles to use. And they have the biggest compost piles because they've killed more plants than anyone else!" There is no shame in killing a plant; there is only shame in doing so repeatedly and blaming it on someone else—or by not learning from the plant's death in the first instance.

How to Pick a Nursery or Garden Center

Picking a good and reliable nursery or garden center is simple—walk in and have a look around. Local nurseries must be your first stop. (Support your community businesses!) You can ask a friend who's been there before to take you there and introduce you to the staff, or just go by yourself.

Bring along a few basic questions to ask so you can get a feeling for the staff, its knowledge, and the way interactions go. Ask about a particular plant—Why does it look this way or that? Will it grow well in my soil and light conditions? You don't have to buy anything. "Just looking" is perfectly acceptable. Asking one or two simple questions is, too.

Note the layout of the nursery. Is it clean and tidy on a quiet day—or a busy day? Expect some untidiness on a busy weekend, Mother's Day weekend (which is the busiest time of the year in the nursery business), or during a spectacular spring when it seems everyone is shopping there and it's all the business can do to wait on customers, restock, and water plants. I will admit to finding amazing, rare, and wonderful plants of good value at tatty nurseries, but it takes years of experience—or a natural instinct—to get to that point. Also keep in mind that during the growing season the business will have the least amount of stock on a Monday after a busy weekend. It often takes three days to order and get in new, fresh stock for the next weekend. Usually by Friday morning all the new stock for the week will be in.

Notice if the plants are clearly labeled—sometimes just with a sign for all the plants or for each individual plant— and if they look healthy. Is there a sense of vibrancy and life to them? They should look moist and plump, like a healthy dog's nose. Are you greeted by a staff person or are you ignored and left to wander? If staff isn't nearby, go into the store and ask for help. Do the staff members behind the counter seem to know their plants or does it feel like they are just there to ring up your sale and take your money? Nothing wrong with that, as long as they can get you a knowledgeable plant person quickly to answer your questions or help you find a plant.

Leave your money at home on your first visit. You don't have to buy anything. You are on a reconnaissance mission. Bring a photo of a part of your garden you want advice on planting. Ask for a quick idea of one or two plants for this site. Remember, this is just a test to see what kind of information and assistance you get, not a real shopping trip. You do not want to be wasting the business's time, nor yours, asking for a detailed site plan right then. That will come later, though you should remember that most nurseries and garden centers do not have a design service and cannot spend half an hour or an hour helping you design your garden.

Good questions to ask

As you ask your questions, do you sense enthusiasm from the staff? Do they actually tell you **not** to buy something because it won't work in your garden's conditions? Having someone talk you out of buying a plant is often a sign of great knowledge and good service. Of course, like you and me, sales staff members have bad days, too, but you should still sense an enthusiasm about a plant when the person is talking to you about it. Try asking the person what her or his "must have" plant is. Listen while the person explains why this plant is so indispensable. Don't express your opinion of the plant—you're trying to figure out the knowledge of the staff member, not waste his or her time with your contradictions, knowledge, or disagreements. You want to hear what he or she has to say to see if this advice feels right for you.

Another good question to ask is what the staff person thinks of a highly advertised new plant. National garden columnists and their television counterparts may not be good judges of which plant is good for your area, even if the local garden center is selling it. You should look to local garden writers and television presenters, who are better suited, in most cases, to understand what grows well or may grow well in your area. New, nationally advertised plants are often for sale at a local nursery because of an artificially created demand or a good wholesale salesperson, not because the plants are good for your area. Customers demand what is advertised, whether it's appropriate for Peoria, St. Petersburg, or Pretoria. It's that simple. Garden store and nursery owners have to walk a fine line between stocking what's in fashion and stocking good plants.

If you are one of those who get your information from advertisements and enjoy novelty, you should still ask the store's staff what the general thinking is about the new star. Chances are you will be given a very informed opinion. If the staff does not have one, then wait a year or two, letting others in the garden world spend their money experimenting on the latest fad. You won't lose points in your garden if it's not filled with the latest and rarest, no matter what the plant snob next door says or what Madison Avenue is promoting at the moment.

Two current examples of plants being promoted as great for any garden—but that aren't necessarily so—are echinacea or coneflowers, and heucheras. Scores of new cultivars are produced each year. But here is the reality: these new, very colorful coneflowers are often bred from naturally short-lived perennial parents that do best in hot, sunny climates with distinct cold periods but not severe winters. If you want a long-lived perennial or can't provide these growing conditions, expect to be disappointed by the plant's performance. Heucheras with their lovely, colorful foliage may have rust disease issues in humid areas or may scorch in hot, dry summers. If, in your garden, both of these plants last for years without disease, enjoy them and revel in the fact that plants do not know what they are or are not supposed to do.

A question that invariably comes up at many a nursery in North America is this: "Do you have a Master Gardener on staff?" In the United States and Canada, Master Gardeners are certified individuals who have attended a series of in-depth gardening classes and seminars and passed a series of exams. These individuals are then required to spend a specified amount of time volunteering at public events where they answer horticultural questions, give advice, and otherwise share what they learned in the program.

Do not be deterred if a nursery does not have a Master Gardener on staff. Master Gardeners provide a fine service, but not all are necessarily versed in the hands-on, practical knowledge and skill that comes only from years of working in gardens and with plants. Some of the best nurseries in the world are staffed with fine horticulturalists who have no certificates or degrees in any horticultural area. What they have is years of practical experience and the wisdom to admit what they don't know. Some are recognized authorities on a particular plant or type of horticulture.

While we are on the topic of questions, here are my learned answers to two of the most common: unequivocally, there is no living ground cover that will grow and survive in a dog run if the dog is larger than a squirrel, nor is there one for a play area used by active children wearing cleats while playing soccer. A well-established, well-maintained lawn—and that's not cheap to have nor a chemical-free area—is good for dogs or children to play on occasionally. But wood and gravel mulched areas or tattered, well-loved, fieldlike lawns are the only places for dogs and kids to play with abandon, as they should. Enjoy both while you can. The time for a perfect lawn will come with astonishingly bittersweet speed.

How to get good service and advice

To get good service, you need to be a good customer. If possible, come prepared with a good-sized piece of the plant (with flowers or fruits) you want to buy for identification, or with photos of your landscape and its measurements, or with an idea—and be prepared to listen carefully. If you don't like what you're hearing, don't be dismissive of the salesperson's suggestions nor argumentative or insulting. That is the quickest way to get a salesperson to agree with anything you say, the equivalent of giving you enough rope to hang your own garden. You want honesty. As fans of Monty Python know, "Arguments are down the hall."

If you don't like or understand what you're hearing and feel like you and the salesperson are not communicating, you have two choices; both involve saying, "Thank you for your time." Then you can leave and go to another nursery, or you can walk around the nursery until you find another salesperson, far away from the first, and ask him or her just one of your questions. If the answer is similar to the first, you should pay attention. If it's markedly different, you should leave and do some book research on your own. Be wary of Internet information—but more on that in the next chapter.

It's so important to remember why you are asking a question: to get good information to help you be a better gardener and to have a healthy garden. Why on earth would you want someone to agree with you when you are possibly wrong or ignorant, or when what you want may not even be possible or in the best interest of your garden or the plant?

A plant is a living thing, like a potential pet. Neither is a piece of furniture you can repaint or put in the attic if it does not work or you find you do not like it.

Here are clear examples of bad advice: anyone telling you that a rose garden will grow well in a woodland, that a cactus is perfect in a wet area by your leaky fountain, that deer do not eat vegetables, that daffodils bloom throughout the summer. Anyone giving you any of these pieces of advice is someone whose advice needs to be submitted for a second opinion. Ask a professional horticulturalist or someone whose garden thrives. But realize that neighborly advice, often with the best intentions, can sometimes be more harmful than helpful. For instance, many well-meaning neighbors will offer you advice on how to make concoctions and home brews of fertilizers, pesticides, soil amendments, and weed killers. But if the instructions make you feel like some sort of medieval alchemist concocting potions in the cellar to create horticultural gold, be wary. Some home remedies are just as toxic as banned chemicals. Nicotine, for example, is horribly toxic, yet I see or hear of homemade brews made from steeped cigarette butts that are then sprayed on plants to kill bugs—and maybe you or your pets. How your neighbor's garden looks is the thing you should be thinking about at this point. If it looks great, listen to the advice. If it doesn't or the advice seems overly complex or it's not your type of garden, go ask a nursery person for advice. Simple advice is usually the best.

And speaking of advice, when you and your spouse or partner come to the nursery, don't come looking for someone to validate **your** opinion over your partner's, or for someone to be a referee between the two of you. For that seek a professional counselor, not nursery staff. They have enough to do keeping up with the watering, answering horticultural questions, selling plants, and keeping peace in their own homes.

Mail-Order Nurseries

A major alternative to local nurseries and garden centers is mail-order nurseries. Practically speaking, there are hundreds of thousands of plants and seeds you can purchase with minimal fuss from mail-order nurseries. A few very small nurseries only offer short catalogs or one-page lists of seeds or plants, but many mail-order nurseries now have websites allowing you to view, choose, and order plants. The Internet has become the primary source to find the plants your local nursery or garden center doesn't have, for whatever reason.

As you will be paying to have the plants shipped to you—sometimes up to 30 percent of the cost of your total order—you may wonder why you would even bother to use a mail-order nursery. The answer is simple: there are thousands of different plants that will never be produced by wholesale growers. The wholesale nurseries are geared to produce and sell plants in mind-bogglingly big numbers. Plants that sell in only the hundreds or even the dozens across the country in any given year or season will not be part of the big wholesaler's business plan. Thus the niche for small—and large—mail-order and family nurseries.

There are brilliant mail-order nurseries specializing in camellias, bulbs, plants for the Rocky Mountains, dwarf conifers, houseplants, plants for the humid South, hostas, alpine plants, seeds from around the world, and annuals. Think of a plant or a category and there is a mail-order nursery for it. Some mail-order nurseries produce short lists of limited numbers of plants, while others are large-scale operations. Search away and know your garden's—and your credit card's—limits. You can print out a catalog you like, or cut and paste the plants that interest you to create a "plant wants list" to carry with you, which is what I do.

The big advantage of mail order is availability. Internet catalogs can be revised quickly as plants become available or sell out. Also, there is more room in an online catalog than on a tag for information about a particular plant. Now that most catalogs are on the Internet, production and mailing costs are eliminated and the savings are passed along to the customer, allowing many small esoteric nurseries to tempt us with amazing plants. (However, I do miss the arrival of mail-order catalogs in the mailbox in January, reading them, making marks and comments in the margins, or keeping them to refer back to years later when a label from a plant has been lost.)

On the other hand, the drawbacks to be aware of when mail ordering plants include delays or problems in shipping, the fact that you can't physically see and select the actual plant you want, and the reality that some plants cannot be shipped to your state or country because of agricultural or customs or international regulations (most mail-order companies know this and tell you straight up if they can't mail to certain areas).

Finding mail-order nurseries

Since most mail-order nurseries have an Internet presence even if they still mail out a printed catalog, a quick search online for "mail-order maples" or "mail-order plant nurseries" will find you what you're looking for or lead you on to other links.

If you are looking for a particular plant, the University of Minnesota's Anderson Horticultural Library maintains a website (www.plantinfo.umn.edu/) updated at least annually of plants listed in printed and online catalogs in the United States. On the website you simply type in the botanical (or common) name of a plant you are looking for; if a nursery in the United States lists it that year, the site will tell you the nursery or nurseries selling it and if it is sold retail or wholesale, and will often direct you to the website(s).

The Royal Horticultural Society in the United Kingdom annually publishes, in book form and also on its website,

Ordering from Other Countries

It's possible to import plants yourself, but familiarize yourself with your country's plant importation requirements and follow them to the letter if you want any chance of success.

Minimally, an import permit is required. In the United States, go to the USDA-APHIS website, look under "plant import permits" or "small seed lots import permits," and follow the instructions to get a permit. You will have to go in person to an office and present government-issued identification to complete the process, but it is much easier and faster than it used to be. Most countries issue import permits to their citizens via the country's agricultural department; in Canada, it's the Canadian Food Inspection Agency, and in the United Kingdom, it's the Department for Environment, Food, and Rural Affairs.

Make sure the other country's mail-order nursery will ship to your country. Import regulations and requirements can be immensely complicated and costly to the exporting nursery, and losses in shipping and during importation inspection can be great, so many nurseries choose not to export. Respect this decision.

Also, it is important to calmly cooperate with your local plant inspector. They are often overworked, tasked with enforcing complicated and seemingly conflicting regulations, and responsible for keeping devastating diseases and insects from entering the coun-

The Plant Finder for nurseries in the United Kingdom, list-ing the plants those nurseries offer. This site can locate the nurseries that offer a plant during the year of publication and also gives a direct link to that nursery's website or an e-mail address. *The Plant Finder* has also become the inter-national authority on correct plant names and spellings. Similar publications and websites exist in other countries. Search them out.

When doing an online search, you may find that some plants are available only from wholesale nurseries, so you, the home gardener, are out of luck. You can ask your local

try. These inspectors have no control over the shipping carrier, cus-toms (which also has to inspect your package), how the nursery packed the plants, or if the nursery of origin included the proper permits. I find the best way to handle any situation that arises is to treat local inspectors with respect, know the laws and regulations, and ask intelligent questions about what you might be able to do next time to avoid the current problem. After all, that is how you would want to be treated in your place of business, is it not?

Over the years I've imported many plants. By carefully follow-ing regulations, managing my expectations, and keeping in con-stant contact with the shipping company about what's required to get the plants to the inspection station quickly, I would say I have had more successes than failures and found the process worth the effort, worry, and expense in the end (though I wouldn't necessar-ily have said that during the process). Others might not think this way. It is all in your expectations and how well you have done your homework.

If you do not want to deal with importation on your own, you can hire plant customs brokers. Search online and expect to pay well for this service. To explore plant importation further, check out your country's laws and regulations under its department of agriculture.

nursery if it can get the plant, but remember that to buy wholesale, a retail nursery has to buy large numbers of the plant and pay for the freight. No nursery can order one small shrub just for you and sell it at a reasonable price when the trucking cost may be a hundred times the original cost of the plant you want.

It is also important to remember that not all walk-in nurseries or garden centers deal with all wholesale nurseries, regardless of what a wholesale nursery may say on its website. If you run into that situation, please don't blame the retail nursery for this misrepresentation by the wholesale nursery. E-mail or call the wholesaler and complain to them. Let them know you want to know who **really** carries the plant you're looking for, not the names of nurseries who the wholesalers would like to carry the product.

Simple searches on the Internet will bring up many mail-order nurseries—but make sure they are ones in your country! Importing plants from other countries is doable but not easy, inexpensive, or logical at times. (See "Ordering from Other Countries.") Regulations change quickly, and government-issued permits are required, as are inspections and fees. The majority of plants being produced and that can grow in your country are more often than not already in your country or soon to be coming in via the big wholesalers. The hard part for you is being patient until these plants enter the marketplace in numbers sufficient to sell or trade, or finding someone who has them and is willing to do either.

How do you know if a mail-order nursery is reputable? Ask friends, check with garden club members, or look at some of the nursery rating sites online. Read the comments—and read carefully between the lines. Some customers are fussy and annoying and have ridiculous expectations—as do some nurseries. Are the ravers or ranters similar to or different from each other? How were problems resolved? I have ordered many plants from nurseries that get rants on these rating websites, yet I've never had a problem because I read the terms of business and note phrases like "difficult plant to grow." In other words, I have managed my expectations and paid attention.

Before you order and when your plants arrive

Before you order, you should read all the fine print, which is important and sometimes humorous. When you find a mail-order nursery that intrigues you, the first thing you always do is run through its plant list marking plants of interest or filling the shopping cart with what you want, when what you should really be doing is reading the terms of business and the instructions on how to order. Many nurseries ship only at certain times of the year or to certain states, and each state has its own laws and regulations regarding the importation of plants. Whether or not such rules seem logical to you, the selling nursery must obey these rules.

Many of the instructions or terms of business are brutally frank. Read them and learn, laugh, or become perturbed. Every business has the right to refuse you service without prejudice. So follow the instructions to the letter. Remember that a plant may sell out by the time your order arrives or is filled. Check online. Many mail-order nurseries update their websites frequently and list which plants are sold out or which new plants are for sale now. Plants die in cold winters or in heat waves or are washed away in floods or blown into Oz by tornados and hurricanes. If a plant is restricted to "one per person," don't order two. Just be patient. In other words, remind yourself that you are dealing with a living thing—and living things do not always behave as you or the grower wants them to.

When the plants arrive, they should be well wrapped, sometimes secured to the box by staples or tape, and with stakes. Each company packs differently. Carefully disassemble all the packing materials and remove the plants from the box. Compare the plants to the invoice to make sure everything is there, noting any that are on back order or were out of stock. If the latter, did you receive a credit or refund?

The plants should be in good shape albeit a bit tired looking (not unlike us after a long plane trip). Don't worry if a leaf or two is bent or withered. This is normal. But do expect the plants to be alive and showing good health. Read and follow any instructions included with the plants. Water and place them in a cool, lightly shaded place for a day or two to recover; then they can be planted out. If the plants seem too small to plant out (some growers do send very young, lightly rooted yet healthy rarities), let them continue to grow in the original pot until large enough to plant out. One of the first signs that a plant is big enough to plant is when you notice the first root or two reaching out the bottom of the pot—that's the time to carefully remove the plant from the pot and put it in the ground.

Problems with your order

If you have a problem with your order, contact the nursery immediately and politely. Have all your paperwork at hand, including your name, address, date of purchase, and any invoice number. Customer service people are not mind readers. If they were, they wouldn't be in the business, rather they would be sitting on yachts off some warm and beautiful coast, not taking calls from customers who forget which time zone they live in and which one the nursery is in.

State plainly what you believe to be the problem: wrong name, wrong size, missing plant, dead plant. Be willing to answer several questions from the customer service person or nursery owner while he or she tries to build a mental picture in order to figure out the problem. It's not an inquisition—just simple fact finding to resolve the problem. Don't take offense. If the customer service person seems to be truly giving you attitude, politely ask to talk to a supervisor, but save that for really difficult situations.

If the box of plants you receive was damaged in shipping, that's not the nursery's fault; read its "terms of business" section on shipping. In this case, first contact the shipper. You cannot hold the nursery responsible for what the shipper did. You can only hold the nursery responsible for how the plants were packed. After contacting the shipper, no matter the outcome, you should contact the nursery and let them know of the problem you had with the shipper. If they get many complaints about a shipper, it's in the nursery's best interest to talk to the shipper or change to another.

I have ordered from around the world. In more than forty years of buying plants by mail order, I have had only one bad experience with a nursery. It charged me for plants I didn't order, sent the wrong ones for those I did order, and never replied to phone calls, letters, or e-mails. It is no longer in business. I have, at times, been a bit disappointed by the size or quality of a plant, but the plant eventually did grow because I paid extra attention to it, and in the end it was worth it. Other times a plant has arrived in pristine condition or larger than I would have hoped. I do my research on the nursery, the laws of importation, and the plant. And I don't expect a rare plant that only one nursery in the world sells to be big, no matter what price I pay.

In the end, remember to take a deep breath and that people make mistakes—at nurseries and in your own home.

Other Plant Sources

Besides retail stores and mail-order nurseries, sources of plants include small non-mail-order nurseries, local sales, and networking. In addition, many county soil and water conservation districts in the United States offer plant starts, often bare root, for sale. You usually need to preorder, and then you can pick up your starts at a designated place and time. Do an Internet search for such sales in your county.

Small non–mail-order nurseries

Many small nurseries are so small that they sell only on-site or at local garden sales, not by mail order—no matter how hard you plead. If several are near each other or on a logical vacation route, map out your plans for a visit, but always call ahead to make sure they are or will be open to visitors when you are coming through. Many such nurseries don't allow people on their property because of insurance, security, or privacy issues. Respect this. How many strangers—with potential sticky fingers or eager lawyers on retainer—would you want tromping around your garden or in your home?

Some of these nurseries can be found online. A polite note or e-mail about visiting may open the garden gate. Always enclose a self-addressed stamped envelope when writing. Profit margins are slim for these little nurseries. And if you are invited in, bring cash to pay for your plants.

Credit card and bank fees can eat into small nursery's profits. Get a receipt, too.

Local sales

Even smaller than family nurseries are local plant sales.

Many garden clubs, garden societies, arboretums, and public and private gardens sponsor annual or twice yearly sales as fund-raisers. Often this will be the only time a small, exquisite nursery will offer a public experience. Come with plenty of cash in your pocket, an informed list, and quick reflexes. Buyers who are old hands at these sales will see and grab a rarity while you are hemming and hawing about the cost, if the name is what you think it should be, or whether the color will match the trim on your windowsill. Better to grab hold of the plant as you look around, then make up your mind after your once-over of the stall or the sale room. If you don't want the plant, put it back from where you got it.

At local sales you often get to talk directly to the grower. Again, come with specific questions and a notebook. Don't waste the vendor's time with indecision or stories about your or your great aunt's prowess in growing plants. Most growers are happy to answer questions if someone is paying attention. If a vendor is not busy and seems chatty, by all means chat away and learn, learn, learn.

Bring cash or your checkbook. Credit card sales, while convenient to you, cost the small grower quite a bit extra in fees. The seller is already paying a large percentage of the plant's price to the sponsoring show organizer, so every penny counts to the grower.

Be prepared for big crowds to arrive before opening time at popular sales. Have a plan of action. The simplest one is to—safely—rush first to the nursery booth you want to visit and then visit the others later. Come with a box or bag, notebook and pen, cash, enthusiasm, patience, and a willingness to learn. Stay until the crowd thins out. Many vendors are mobbed by customers and can't get around to restocking and reorganizing until things quiet down. It's amazing what you can find at such a time.

Networking

Many specialist plant societies have sales that small nurseries selling rarities attend. These societies often facilitate exchanges of plants and seeds among members or will get you in touch with members willing to trade or sell a plant. However, never expect to just pop off an e-mail or letter and immediately get a very rare plant. You should inquire first if the person ever trades or sells the plant. Offer what you might have to trade in the case of the former or ask what the person is looking for that you might be able to supply from some small non-mail-order nursery in your area. When asking, always be polite, sincere, and realistic. Don't be demanding, which will always put you at the top of the "never gonna happen" list. At best you can hope the gardener or nursery will put you on a waiting list only a few years in length.

3

How to Read a Plant Tag or Catalog Description

It's time to start choosing plants. The first piece of hard information you're going to encounter is on the tag stuck in the plant's container, on a sign, or in a catalog description. (In this chapter when I say *tag*, I mean to include tags, signs, and catalog descriptions.) What does the tag tell you? And what doesn't it tell you? A good tag should have the botanical name, maybe a common name, a brief description of the plant, its star qualities, and its basic needs.

Many good small nurseries have neither the time nor the money to print out elaborate labels, which often get misplaced on plants in the nursery. At such nurseries you may even be asked to write out your own label. Perfectly reasonable. Buy the nursery's descriptive list or catalog filled with more descriptions and information than could ever be put on a label. These are valuable reference works. Read them, keep them, learn from them, and write out your own label. It'll help you start setting the name in your brain.

All of the various words and terms found on tags and in plant descriptions are important for you to be familiar with and to understand in order to make appropriate choices of plants and in designing your garden. It is also important for you to remember that it is the goal of the nursery to sell you its plants. You also hope these are plants suited for your area. When you understand words and phrases commonly used on tags and in descriptions, or in a staff person's explanation of a plant's needs and habits, you will be able to make good choices. Ask for clarification if you don't understand—there is no shame in doing so since it's the way you learn. And take notes! Don't expect that you will remember much of anything said to you during your discussion. You waste your own and the nursery person's time if you keep asking to have repeated what was just said. Plus, writing notes actually helps imprint them in your memory.

Why Is a Tag/Description Important?

The first reason a tag is important is that you will need it if there is a problem with the plant and you have to return it. Businesses need proof of purchase, and the label that came with the plant is the best form, along with the sales slip, which will often have the only indication of the price you paid.

The second reason a tag is important is for the information on it, the most important piece being the plant's name. Save the tag for your records. Get a large manila envelope and use it to store tags from each kind of plant you buy

Save plant tags for your records. If you organize them into lists or manila envelopes by year, they will be easy to refer to when you can't remember a plant's name or you want to give a plant away with information to orient the new owner.

during the year. At the end of the year, you can do one of two things. You can make a list of each of the tags, maybe even noting where the plant was planted, whether you liked it or not, and any other performance issues, successes, or failures. Or you can simply seal up the envelope, mark it with the year, and put it in a file or box with the previous years' envelopes for future reference.

Believe me, you will forget the name of the most fantastic plant in your garden, the one that all of your neighbors and friends will want to know about. And if you ever peruse the labels or your lists, you will be surprised to find out how many plants you have killed over and over. In all instances it will make you a better gardener and, better yet, make you sound like a knowledgeable one.

Botanical Name

A good plant tag or catalog description should tell you the plant's proper botanical name—the unpronounceable Latin one. Common names vary from country to country, town to town, neighbor to neighbor. Botanical names are universal, even though science does make continual changes, but that's not important here as those changes often take time to be adopted and to trickle down to your local nursery's plant label.

Don't be afraid of speaking the botanical name. Pronunciations may differ, but not the spelling. If you know what

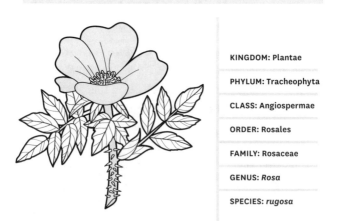

KINGDOM: Plantae

PHYLUM: Tracheophyta

CLASS: Angiospermae

ORDER: Rosales

FAMILY: Rosaceae

GENUS: *Rosa*

SPECIES: *rugosa*

Rosa rugosa

Botanical taxonomy sorts every plant into a series of categories from very general to very specific and labels it with the genus and species name.

Rosa, Iris, Rhododendron, Delphinium, Lupinus, Aster, Chrysanthemum, Poinsettia, Tulipa, Dahlia, Lobelia, and Alyssum are, you are already familiar with botanical names. Did you catch the three that are slightly different—Rosa, Lupinus, and Tulipa? But you still knew what they were.

Common names are often arbitrary. One name may be used for several very different plants: a japonica can be a pieris, a quince, or an azalea, to name just a few. A syringa is not a lilac, even though Syringa is its botanical name. Syringa as a common name refers to Philadelphus, which shares its other common name, mock orange, with a host of differing plants, temperate and tropical. See how confusing common names can be? This is why we need the botanical name. When a nursery person asks you questions about which japonica or mock orange you're inquiring about, he or she is not trying to make you feel ignorant or stupid. The goal is to make sure you get the correct answer and the correct plant.

A good tag will have the full botanical name, which is made up of the genus, the species, and the cultivar name (if there is one), in that order. For example, the name Aster cordifolius 'Chieftain' contains all three. The genus is Aster. The particular species is cordifolius, and this cultivar is a special form given the proper name of 'Chieftain', always in the single quotation marks. This use of single quotation marks tells you that all such named plants are identical, created from divisions or cuttings taken from the original plant. This is cloning as it has been done for tens of thousands of years. Every plant so labeled will be the same. Some plants from the same seed strain that look identical may also be called cultivars even though they are not clonally propagated; their breeding line is so pure that all offspring are essentially identical.

Botanical taxonomy is, simply put, humans' way of sorting out the natural world in the name of science. It is a system established and clarified by the eighteenth-century Swedish scientist Carl Linnaeus, giving every living thing at least two names, much like the Western cultural personal naming systems of a first and a last name for each person. Modified over the years, the system is still simple and brilliant in its approach. (This is putting it very simply but in a practical way for the average gardener to understand. If you want more knowledge, there are hundreds of books on the subject to occupy you for as much time as you have left on this celestial orb.)

As a little more explanation, let's call a genus the last name of the plant, even though it comes first. It is the group to which many species belong. *Aster* is a genus. All asters are botanically and conveniently called *Aster*, which derives from the Greek for star—and don't asters look like little stars? But we often see that many wild asters in different areas look distinct from each other—subtly or obviously— yet they still look like an aster. If individuals within these different groups breed only with their similar kinds and the resulting offspring continue to look exactly like the parents, they are, simply put, a species—the equivalent of a first name. So the species (which is also what the combination of the genus and species names is called) *Aster cordifolius* is a recognized, interbreeding group of asters that look the same, within reasonable bounds. The species name, cordifolius, means heart-shaped foliage or leaf.

Occasionally, differences in flower color, plant size, or leaf color occur. These are naturally occurring forms or mutations that happen in the wild or in nursery seed pots. Most never survive long in nature, but gardeners, always looking

for novelty, coddle and propagate these aberrations hop-
ing one or all will be seen as beautiful and desirable. Such
forms or mutations are then given "cultivar" names—the
word is an abbreviated combination of the words cultivated variety—to denote that it is we, not nature, who have
selected and cultivated this oddity, keeping it alive where
nature most likely would have let it die out.

Genus and species names are usually written in italics
according to convention. The International Code of Botanical Nomenclature, which governs the scientific naming of
plants, does not, as is presumed, require this. It has simply
become a common practice based on the English and American literary convention of italicizing foreign words. Since
Linnaeus's system used Latin and classical Greek words,
they are considered foreign. The cultivar name, unitalicized,
is put in single quotation marks to signify a clone or seed
strain. If double quotation marks are used, this means the
name is either a common name or a working name until a
real name is coined or one is discovered for a found plant
presumed to be an old, lost cultivar. And if the cultivar name
or seed collection number is in brackets—for example,
['Betsy'] or [DJHC96002]—as some nurseries recently have
done, this means the plant was grown from seed of a normally clonally propagated cultivar, so who knows what or
who the mature plant will look like. Surprise ensues!

Common Name

But what is a plant's common name? you insist. Okay, I'll
tell you. In the case of the previously mentioned *Aster cordifolius* 'Chieftain', its common name is "the plant with the
heart-shaped leaf and the star-flower called Chieftain." An
easy one. Here's a tougher one. Meadow rue is a common

name in the English-speaking world for what is botanically *Thalictrum*. So a thalictrum is a meadow rue—fair enough. But when people insist that they want the common name for *Thalictrum rochebrunianum* 'Lavender Mist', I very much enjoy telling them, "Oh, yes, you mean 'Herr Baron von Rochebrun's meadow rue that looks like lavender-colored mist'." Now really, which would you rather learn and say?

Most common names are just loose translations of the botanical name. Botanical names may be related to the appearance of the flower or foliage, though not always, since botanists are always reexamining and changing plant names until the name no longer describes the plant it was originally attached to. Worldwide, very few plants have common names, as the majority of plants remain wild and have never been cultivated and given common names other than "that red flower in the mountains" or "that tall yellow thing by the stream."

Plant Type

The tag or catalog description should tell you if the plant is an annual, a biennial, a perennial, a shrub, a subshrub, a tree, a bulb, or a vine or climber.

ANNUAL. The word annual means that the individual plant grows from seed, flowers, sets seed, and dies in one year. These plants are technically monocarpic, meaning once-fruiting (mono = one or once; carpic = fruit/fruiting). Most modern strains and cultivars of annuals bloom all summer long, until frost or sheer exhaustion ends their short lives.

HARDY OR TENDER ANNUAL. Sometimes a plant is called a hardy or a tender annual. The former means the plant can tolerate and thrive in cold temperatures, even germinating in near-freezing weather, like peas or spinach, to name two hardy annuals. Tender annuals, on the other hand, must have very warm air and soil temperatures to germinate and thrive—think watermelons and corn.

BIENNIAL. A biennial is a plant that lives two years, blooming, seeding, and dying at the end of the second year. It is also a monocarpic, or once-fruiting, plant. Many monocarpic plants may live for three or four years or one hundred before flowering only one time, setting seed, and then promptly dying (the century plant comes to mind). Biennial means two years.

PERENNIAL. A perennial is a plant that grows, flowers, and sets seed for several years. Sometimes it lives for centuries or sometimes just for three or four years, but it flowers and sets seed more than two years. A short-lived perennial, like many echinacea, may naturally live for just three to five years. The word perennial simply means lasting for a long or indefinite time.

TENDER PERENNIAL. You will often come across plants labeled as tender perennials. What this term means is that in its native climate such a plant is a perennial, living for years, but your climate is too wet or cold—or some other weather-related superlative—for the plant to survive from year to year. Usually it means it's too cold where you live. Zonal geraniums (correctly pelargoniums) are tender perennials. In their native frost-free lands they are often semi-woody plants becoming shrubs over time, but in areas of hard winter frosts or freezes they are toast (a mixed but easily understood metaphor), thus treated as an annual—even though they may, perhaps, just survive outdoors from year to year in regions of light frost, such as the Pacific Northwest. I hope you noticed all the qualifiers in the last part of that sentence!

SHRUB. A shrub is usually a woody plant with many stems coming from near or below ground level. The woody stems remain alive and grow longer from year to year. A shrub can be deciduous or evergreen. (See "Does It Keep or Lose

Does It Keep or Lose Its Leaves?

The plant tag or catalog description of a shrub or tree will say if the plant is evergreen or deciduous. You may also see or hear the terms *semi-deciduous*, *semi-evergreen*, *herbaceous*, and *semi-herbaceous*. It's important to know what these terms mean so your expectations are in line with reality.

A *deciduous* plant loses its leaves once a year. It's not dead when this happens. It's dormant, incapable of making new growth due to cold temperatures, hot temperatures, low sunlight, or drought. Most deciduous leaves are wide and flat like a maple leaf, though some trees with needle-shaped leaves are deciduous—larch and dawn redwoods, to name two. These needle-leaved deciduous plants frighten new gardeners come autumn when they drop their needles in a glory of autumnal yellows or rusts, causing the gardener to think the plant has died. Knowing a plant is supposed to drop its leaves will save you a moment of panic.

An *evergreen* plant retains its current year's leaves as well as the past year's or even leaves a few years older. It does, however, always shed its oldest leaves, sometimes in spring, sometimes in summer, sometimes in autumn. It's a good thing to know which of these seasons it will do its shedding if the plant is to be placed in the middle of a patio or near a pool where fallen leaves will create a problem. As long as the leaves are being shed from the interior of the plant or from a part of a branch closest to the main stem or trunk, this is normal. If the leaves are shedding from the tips of the branches, something's wrong. Time to visit your nursery or garden center for advice. Not all evergreen plants are conifers, with

Its Leaves?") Some shrubs can be trained as small trees, which are called standards.

SUBSHRUB. The term subshrub is a rarely used but still seen enough to warrant inclusion. It means a shrublike plant that has stems that may die back part way toward the soil or just below the soil during the dormant season either naturally or due to colder temperatures. Russian sage

needle-shaped leaves like a pine or spruce—a Christmas tree. There are broadleaf evergreens: evergreen magnolias (obvious from the name), camellias, most rhododendrons, most hollies, mountain laurels, and boxwood, just to name a few.

The terms *semi-deciduous* and *semi-evergreen* are brain busters and often used to mean the same thing, but they don't. A semi-deciduous plant always loses most but not all of its leaves in its natural environment. A semi-evergreen plant holds on to at least half of its leaves in its native lands. In the gardening world, since they are used synonymously, consider them to mean this: come a very cold winter or a summer drought, the majority of the leaves will fall off or stay on, depending on how severely the plant reacts to the climatic conditions.

Herbaceous refers to perennials, bulbs, and some vines that die down to resting buds at or below ground level during the dormant season. No top growth remains living aboveground once the plant goes dormant. If some of the plant, but less than half, remains alive aboveground during the dormant season, the term for this is *semi-herbaceous*. The plant dies part way to the ground because that is how it has evolved or that is how it responds to severe or even mild weather conditions. Such perennials may retreat to a crown or rosette of leaves at ground level in the winter, like heucheras and some campanulas. The Itoh hybrid peonies—hybrids between tree peonies and herbaceous peonies—are either herbaceous or semi-herbaceous, depending on which parent's gene is dominant and how harsh the winter was.

(*Perovskia*) and some elderberries (*Sambucus*) are considered subshrubs.

TREE. A tree is a woody-stemmed plant with one central stem or trunk with branches emerging several feet above ground level. Some trees may be cut down early in their lives to regrow multiple trunks or stems near ground level, but that is not their natural inclination. Trees, like shrubs, can be evergreen or deciduous.

BULB. In common but not botanical usage, a bulb is any plant that dies back to an underground swollen storage unit with potential growing points for the next season's growth to emerge. Think of an onion, which is a true bulb in the botanical sense, having swollen leaves (all those rings) underground full of food for new growth and protectively surrounding the next season's growing point. All such plants are technically called xerophytes. We gardeners would lump all of these together as bulbs: corms (such as crocus), tubers (like potatoes or dahlias), rhizomes (bearded iris), and a few other types of these underground storage units.

VINE OR CLIMBER. This is a plant—annual, biennial, perennial, or woody—that produces long, lax growths that either cling to, wind around, or grow over the tops of other plants to find light, or that run about on top of the ground in search of bright areas or fresh soils. Ivies, sweet peas, climbing hydrangeas, most clematis, some jasmine—all are vines of a sort.

Plant Description

A plant tag will always tell you the plant's size, and it may also mention fragrance or lack thereof, color (in the eye of the tag's writer), and, rarely, whether a plant has been grafted. These are important considerations as you contemplate the design of your garden.

Potential size

The size for annuals given on a tag or in a catalog description is usually the height and the planting space width. The latter is also how wide the plant is expected to become under normal growing conditions, just as the height is the expected height under normal growing conditions. You can plant closer together if you want to fill up a space faster. When professionals plant annuals, they often do so at half the recommended planting width, and then after a while they pull out every other plant as the plants grow and come near to touching. This makes for a quick full-planting look over a long season.

As with annuals, biennials have a height and spacing width indicated. So treat them exactly as you would annuals when it comes to their spacing and your height expectations. However, do expect biennials to take at least a year or slightly more to reach mature girth and stature.

For perennials, the height and width given is for an established plant, which usually means a plant that has been in the ground for two or more years (hostas take up to five or more years to reach their maximum). It is the expected maximum size of the plant under normal growing conditions when fully matured. Any perennial labeled creeping, spreading, or running just keeps getting wider and wider, sometimes dying out at ground zero over time. Many clump-forming perennials, like those in the daisy or iris families, grow in ever-expanding clumps with the center part becoming woody and also dying out. Left alone, they will eventually break the circle of growth and become scattered-looking clumps. Once one of these clump formers makes a well-defined ring, it is time for you as gardener and artist to step in and dig out a wedge of the ring—like a slice of cake. From this wedge, keep the outer portion of fresh new growth and throw out the dead-tired center. Give away or replant elsewhere the remaining other fresh parts of the ring. Replant your smaller piece in the hole after filling it with fresh, enriched soil, beginning the process all over.

When the height of a perennial begins to diminish or the plant otherwise weakens after several years, this is most commonly a sign that the plant is congested at the roots, needing division and new, enriched soil. Do as recommended in the previous paragraph—divide and replant in refreshed soil.

For trees and shrubs, unless otherwise **explicitly** stated, the size on the tag is the growth made in ten years (per decade)—not in its lifetime. This horticultural industry standard is based on the real estate industry's standard that the average family lives in a house from seven to ten years. After I explain this to customers, many think that the tree will not grow any bigger after ten years have passed. I tell them to do the math: if it says ten feet in ten years, it means ten feet multiplied by each decade of life: ten feet times five decades equals fifty feet; ten feet by ten decades equals a hundred feet. It is surprising how many customers and nursery staff find it hard to understand that trees don't stop growing after ten years, or ever. They may slow down after accumulating some maturity, but ever the optimists, trees and a few shrubs continue reaching for the stars until gravity, wind, lightning, or a chainsaw brings them down.

Most trees and shrubs do reach a somewhat static height

in time, programmed in their genes. Then the weight of all the growth out at the tips responds to gravity, as does the body weight of members of my own clan, and thus begins the sagging and a general increase in girth until mortal collapse ends it all.

Luckily, most shrubs that threaten to get too big or wide are often easy to prune back or cut down—and all can be dug up and replaced. Do not, however, think that by simply cutting back the top of a **tree** that you will stop it from growing too big. If that's your goal, you have purchased the wrong plant. Cutting back the tip growth to maintain a stable height only works if you are making a hedge and using a plant that responds well to having its top cut back by producing lots of thick side branches—think of yews, beeches, hawthorns, and the like. Yes, the romantic rues and avenues of Paris are lined with trees cut back to a trunk eight to twelve feet tall, stems ending in knobby, clublike growths (*pollarded* is the term used to describe trees pruned like this). But, well, just don't go there in your garden. It looks much better in Paris. In your own garden, choose the proper-sized tree for your yard and wait, or cut down a too-big tree and start over. There's no disgrace in cutting down a tree. We'd not have lumber, pencils, lovely salad bowls, or chopsticks if we didn't—but we might just have a tree falling on our house.

Scents and fragrance

We expect our roses to have fragrance. Knowing this, breeders and sellers tend to describe a nearly scentless rose as having a "mild scent." Bosh! Breeders and sellers of other flowers have picked up on this cheat. Do not expect any fragrance from such flowers. A flower described as having a "light scent" just *might* reward you with one if you stick your nose deep into the flower on a hot day. "Modest fragrance" means the same thing. For a truly fragrant flower, look for words like perfumed, old rose, rich, deep, wide ranging, and the simple but accurate highly scented.

It is important to remember that some flowers release their scent to mix with the surrounding air so that the scent only expresses itself two or three feet away from the flower.

Words That May Be Red Flags

Learn to recognize words in plant descriptions that may be red flags. Here's a list of the most common:

» VIGOROUS, SPREADING, STOLONIFEROUS, OR INCREASES QUICKLY: The plant is a weed at best, a thug at worst. A weed is simply any plant in the wrong place. If you want something to put on a barren hillside in the back forty, this may be the plant for you, but not for your two-foot-square annual bed.

» DIFFICULT: This means "Don't complain to our nursery if it dies within a year; it's even hard for us to grow!" You should expect to kill two or three of these before you figure out the right way to grow them in your garden—or that you can't grow them at all. This kind of plant requires skill, thoughtful research, experience, or just plain luck. There are also times when we can all be thankful that such plants can't read the books and don't know that they are supposed to be difficult—or easy, for that matter — and flourish away in blissful ignorance.

» SLOW GROWER: This is a relative term. It means that in its native environment or at the nursery, the plant doesn't grow fast. The same should be true in your garden, so manage accordingly. However, on rare occasions you'll have a little microclimate that does everything for the plant that it could ever need. Then, whoosh!—you've got a big 'un in the yard. Be delighted and enjoy it if you have the room. Otherwise, call an arborist or heavy equipment company to either cut it down or bulldoze it out.

» DWARF: The plant is not necessarily going to be small or tiny in comparison to the person buying it. "Dwarf" means small in

This makes for great fun when trying to find the source of such a fragrance. The air is filled with it but each flower you smell is scentless until, perhaps, you gently breathe hot air on it to release more of its scent. There are those plants that only release their scent in the evening—night-scented stocks, angel's trumpet (*Brugmansia*), and others. You'll be working in the garden or sitting on the patio on a warm summer's eve and find yourself quickly engulfed by a rich, exotic

comparison to a normal version of the original plant it seeded or mutated from. A dwarf redwood could still be fifty feet tall, while a dwarf rose will probably be only six to ten inches tall. Sometimes a dwarf plant was found as a mutant branch on a normal-sized tree. Cuttings were taken from this branch and are expected to grow into a plant that retains its small stature. But the potential to revert to the size of its parent is always there, so if one year you notice a vigorous stem or branch romping away, get in there and rip—don't cut—it off cleanly from where it originates. If you cut it off, you'll simply make it come back double. By ripping it off cleanly you remove all the cells that have the potential to regrow more branches.

» **NEEDS STAKING, SWAYS IN THE WIND, OR HAS A HEAVY FLOWER HEAD:** Be aware that you will need to stake this plant or place it among shrubs or other sturdy plants to keep it upright. Or you can cut the plant back by half in late spring to make it grow a bit shorter, bushier, and sturdier, a move the British call the Chelsea chop to acknowledge that the time to do this coincides with the Chelsea Flower Show, which is held in late May. If you want to stake the plant, start before it is very tall and use sturdy stakes of an appropriate length—usually tall enough to tie the flower stalk to. A stake that's shorter, just high enough to reach the base of the flower spike or head, will inevitably cause the flower head to snap off in a heavy rain or wind. The stake should also have a good foot or so of length in the ground to be stable enough to hold up the plant.

fragrance. It is magical and a thing well worth considering when designing a garden. The fragrance of angel's trumpet and a bottle of wine shared with guests will soon fill the evening with laughter and joie de vivre, as the flower's scent is actually intoxicating, but since the plant in all parts is very poisonous, don't mix it in the salad!

Many flowers need a warm day—and you a warm nose, especially in winter—before you will notice a fragrance. Thankfully, many winter-flowering plants like daphnes, mahonias, witch hazels, and sweet box (*Sarcococca*) will produce their perfume in temperatures barely above freezing.

Hawthorns and mountain ash (*Sorbus*) have to some a lovely fragrance. I find their scent disgusting, rather like cat food gone off. Yet I like the smell of privet and find a lovely fragrance in its relatives—the villosa types of lilacs, which my hawthorn-and-ash-loving friends can't stand or even smell at times. It seems we humans have at least two noses offered to us during conception. I prefer the one I blindly chose.

In the end, scent is rather a subjective matter. When in doubt, smell the flower on a warm day and make your own decision.

Color descriptions

The front of a plant tag typically contains a photo showing the plant's flowers and foliage as they appear at maturity. Color photographs are created at the mercy of the erratic capabilities of the printer's machine and often fade in the sun, while color naming is subjective at best. View with skepticism and embrace with caution. Here are some suspect color words: *blue*, *lilac*, *rose red*, *red*, *gold*, and *white*. It is surprising how many people pick a color at the nursery while wearing sunglasses that they don't wear at home, where they wonder why the color no longer looks like it did at the nursery.

There are few true blue flowers; some lobelias, delphiniums, poppies, and gentians are true blue. But most of the time the term blue is nursery-speak for bluish lavender or mauve. The same with the term lilac. True lilac should have a good undertone of purple in it. Lavender is a true tint of purple and should be a rich color closer to purple than lilac, not washy or faded. Just think of the flower color of its namesake. Clematis flowers are often described as blue and red, but most are neither, instead falling in the lilac or mauve or purple tints.

Some leaves described as blue are blue (some grasses, for instance) while most are actually bluish, the result of a waxy covering creating either a bluelike color or a pale grayish color that has the effect in the garden of the cool look of blue. This covering is easily removed when an oil or soap-based spray accidentally hits the leaves, as it has on a few occasions in my experience, resulting in a spotty-leaved plant for the rest of the season.

Purple leaves can enrich a color scheme or look dull and leaden, especially if the so-called purple is more brown or the patinated-copper color so often described as purple. A good purple leaf is really the color of mulberries and correctly called murrey, but, sadly, no one uses that very accurate term much, if at all, anymore.

ROSE RED—is there a more abused color term? I think not. It usually means a red with a lot of blue in it, not the true, pure red associated with barns or fire engines or a paint box. The use of the simple word *red* is much corrupted, too. Expect all different varieties of red, but rarely true red. The same applies when the term is used to describe a leaf, which is more likely to be of a pinkish purple tone. Rose and rhododendron color descriptors must be decided upon by some mysterious colorblind committee. I've rarely seen a true red nor ever a blue rose. Rhododendrons come closer to red and blue, though few ever hit the latter spot on. The industry has some strange belief that lavender, mauve, crimson, scarlet, and fuchsia are not popular colors, yet these are the colors of some of the most popular of rhododendrons and roses even if called blue, purple, or red.

GOLD is a color word used all the time for flowers and leaves. It is an inaccurate word. The term is so commonly misused that you should read it to mean a bright, somewhat light egg-yolk yellow. Gold is a shiny metal. I don't know of any flower that has true gold flowers—that is, flowers looking like shiny gold metal. Some yellows looked glazed or lacquered like those of the weedy creeping buttercup

A Simple Technique for Using Color in a Design

If unsure about using or mixing colors in the garden, I fall back on a simple technique taught me by Graham Stuart Thomas: use the color red as your reference. He said to keep any colors that are on the blue side of red (crimson, purple, and blue) away from those colors on the yellow side of red (scarlet into oranges and yellows). Very simple and it works. Yellows and blues, at the far poles from either side of red, go very well together. Attach the two extremes and you get green and the color wheel. What Graham Thomas did was put red at the top and work on either side of that color until reaching green. One could work from green on either side to red and come up with the same effect.

I do think the color wheel, dismissed by some as artificial, is still a very good tool for the beginner. All attempts at creating color schemes, contrasts, and harmonies in the garden are artificial. After all, nature doesn't consult a colorist, working instead on the principle of what grows best where. Color is important only if it brings in the right pollinators.

Ranunculus repens. Calling a flower or leaf gold is a lazy way to describe bright yellow, chartreuse, or orangey yellow. Yes, such yellows may read as golden in evening light, but that's an effect from the light, not the pigment in the flowers. Perhaps *golden* is a better choice. One color that does have a metallic quality to it can be found on the bark of some cherries, especially the Amur chokecherry, *Prunus maackii*. It is truly the color of a shiny new copper penny or well-scrubbed copper-bottomed French saucepan. This chokecherry's bark is remarkable and perhaps singular in the plant world. *Pewter*, denoting a metal that is rarely shiny, is a good word to describe the grayish leaves of many plants.

WHITE, in flower or leaf, can mean anything from a warm ivory shade or creamy milk color to a washed-out or soiled white to the palest blush of pink or the cool blue-white of skim milk. I may sound overly fussy, but each of these whites

The color wheel with its circular gradation of colors blending from one into the other, and with complements across from each other, gives an understanding of how colors might work, or not, with each other if you don't have a natural flair or confidence for using color. If you have these talents, mix your palette as you wish and never mind the neighbors and their comments.

Of course, any rule can be broken once you know how it works. It's nothing more than a starting point, really: a way of understanding, building confidence, and then moving on to your own sense of color and style. Christopher Lloyd, another great English gardener, avoided the color wheel and all sorts of rules to create vibrant, dissonant, and what some called shocking or appalling color combinations. He was in some ways using color like a jazz musician—improvising and stretching the vibrancy of opposing or clashing colors on the wheel to create a beautiful dissonance.

looks very different in sun, in shade, or next to each other or other colors. If you are planning a white garden, you should know which whites you are dealing with so your garden doesn't end up looking like a clothesline hung with dirty linen. Make a bouquet of all the white flowers you plan to use before planting them. This way you will discover which go better together or need to be separated with green- or gray-foliaged plants.

Grafted plants

What does it mean when a tag says that a plant is grafted? Many plants that are a result of mutations—cultivars, to use the correct term mentioned earlier—can't be grown from cuttings. They are incapable of making roots or do so slowly and weakly, so a scion (a stick of the piece of the plant wanted) or bud must be grafted (or spliced) onto another plant called the understock, which is usually a seedling of the same genus, though not always. In other instances, especially with fruit trees, the top is grafted onto a special dwarfing rootstock, which keeps the plant from growing beyond a specific height so that the fruit is easier to harvest or the tree is better suited for small backyard gardens. Grafting is also used in large production nursery operations to quickly produce uniform plants by the tens of thousands.

The understock upon which the cultivar is grafted often sprouts its own stems, which can overwhelm the desired plant grafted on top until it is weakened and dies. You lose the plant you purchased. This is a common occurrence with roses. One day you are puzzled to notice that your four-foot-tall rosebush with large double white flowers is now eight feet tall and sporting small clusters of single pink flowers. The plant has not magically morphed overnight, as many people would believe. What has happened is that the understock has sent up a shoot from underground, unnoticed by you for a couple of years until it has more vigor and size than the plant you bought. To save the top-grafted plant, you must dig down to where this rootstock stem originates from the understock, cut off all but a foot or so of it, then use the claw of a hammer to rip off the rest of the thug's stump from its place of origin. This removes the small circle of stem tissue that produces new buds at its origin from the rootstock. Fill in the hole with dirt and let the wound heal on its own. With a little vigilance you should have your original plant back.

You can tell if a plant is grafted by looking at the base. In the case of a graft, you will notice that the bottom part of

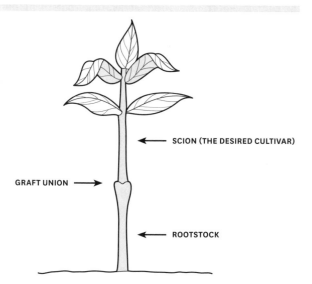

SCION (THE DESIRED CULTIVAR)

GRAFT UNION

ROOTSTOCK

Many cultivars can't be grown well from cuttings and need to be grafted onto the rootstock of another plant. The desired cultivar, called the scion, usually joins the rootstock some inches above the soil level in the nursery pot.

the stem just above soil level is thicker, or bulging, while the trunk above is thinner, thicker, or even has a different color of bark, as often seen on Japanese maples. One or two sprouts may be growing from below this lower, thicker, area or bulge, which is the understock's attempt to be the uber-stock. Crabapples, cherries, witch hazels, and tree dogwoods are some of the most common plants that have vigorous, suckering understock.

The best way to keep these kinds of plants from suckering is to plant them so this understock is completely below ground level, as this deprives the dormant buds of the light they need to switch them on. This is not a foolproof technique (and there is an exception: you don't want to bury the graft union—the union of the understock and the cultivar—of trees grafted on dwarfing rootstock), but it helps. Roses have no problem being planted this way, nor do rose relatives such as apples, crabapples, cherries, mountain ash (Sorbus), and flowering plums. These you can plant with the graft union just below ground level, as long as the graft union is only an inch or so above the roots. I've done this myself on the advice of Graham Thomas. However, too many plants today are grafted much too high, with up to a foot of understock stem, to do this. To plant that graft below ground level on nearly all plants (save roses) will cause rotting and eventually death. This high grafting is an annoying result of modern nursery techniques more convenient to growers than gardeners.

When purchasing a grafted plant, look at the graft union to be sure that it is fully healed, that the top portion is not overwhelming the understock, and that the understock is not sprouting a mass of shoots. That way you will avoid future problems. If the grafted area is not fully healed, this increases the potential for the understock to take over and outgrow the cultivar, killing it. With the exception of roses, when the top portion overwhelms the understock like a big swelling, sagging blob of warm wax, this suggests an incompatibility that could cause the graft to fail sometime in the near or far future. The top will simply break off at the graft union, leaving you with only the rootstock and a dead shrub or tree. It's not a good situation for the long term. If you're only interested in having the plant for a decade or two, you probably won't care, as it may take that long for the damage to do its deed.

If you have questions about the graft union, ask a staff person for his or her opinion. I would advise you not to buy any plant where the top part of the graft is overwhelming the understock. Such plants should have been returned to the grower the moment they arrived at the nursery.

Other descriptors

Many plant descriptions use the terms *standard*, *favorite*, or *rare*.

» **Standard** (here not referring to the method of growing a shrub on a single treelike stem) means the plant is relatively easy to grow and provides color, screening, or beauty with little fuss. It is a plant seen often in gardens and worth seeking out. Standard plants are usually carried by most general nurseries, but they may also become so common and easy to propagate by home gardeners that they are no longer in commercial demand and thus are not feasible for a nursery to grow or sell. If you see a plant growing in gardens all over town but are unable to find it in nurseries and garden centers, this may be why. Ask the owner of the garden how to get a piece. Usually you'll be sent home with one and simple instructions for propagating it.

» *Favorite* means the grower has come to appreciate what the plant does or doesn't do and the beauty it brings to the garden year after year. It may not be easy to grow, but it is well worth growing. This is usually a time-tested plant since nursery growers and sellers don't keep plants around that they can't sell or that cause them trouble.

» *Rare* means rare to the area. It may be quite common in its native land or other gardening areas but not where you live—and it may be easy or difficult to grow. Ask. Or throw all caution to the wind and try it.

Cultural Requirements

There isn't a lot of room on most tags, so descriptions and requirements are minimal or notated with symbols. I find that many of the "internationally understood" symbols are often very difficult to interpret. Ask a staff person for help. The same goes if there is little or no cultural information on the tag. This is when you begin to learn who on staff—or which nursery—really knows plants. You can also augment tag information with catalog descriptions or ask to use the books in the store's reference library if it has one.

Another good source of information is the Internet. I see many customers doing quick informational searches on their smartphones while looking at plants—but I would always ask a staff person if he or she agrees with what you have found on the Internet. In this way you'll begin to understand if a website is useful—or fanciful. The staff person may even be able to recommend a better site for you, whether the nursery's or another's.

At a minimum, a tag should tell you whether a plant needs sun, shade, or either one; moist or dry soils; the generally accepted climate zone the plant is hardy to; and protection from wind. It may also say if a plant specifically needs acidic or alkaline soils.

The tag should also tell you if the plant has a particular requirement in your area. For instance, many cold-hardy gardenias now developed may be truly cold hardy but only if they get lots of summer heat—not sun. So in cool-summer areas a tag should clearly state that the gardenia needs summer heat. In warmer climates a lilac may need several weeks of cold temperatures below a certain degree during dormancy to set flower buds for the following year. Unfortunately, big wholesale growers don't put that information on their tags since they sell all over the country or world. This is when you look for the local independent nursery that either writes its own tags to replace the grower's or has signs posted by the plants giving information applicable to your area. I would lean toward trusting the locally made label over a mass-market one if they contradict. Read the labels and signs carefully. If you still have questions, ask a staff person.

Sun/shade requirements

A plant labeled as needing sun is a plant that relishes full sun all or most of the day. If "full sun" is specified, then full it is. A plant needing full sun must be planted in an area where sunlight, whether in full force or through clouds (cloud cover does not count as shade), is not obstructed by trees, buildings, or parked RVs. Consider eight hours of full sun a day the minimum. Any less and the plant may not flower or grow normally, or it may even die.

The phrase "sun to shade" confuses many people. It is

shorthand meaning that the plant will grow in full sun all day, or in full shade all day, or any variation in between; in other words, the plant is not fussy when it comes to light requirements. "Sun to shade" does not mean that the plant is unable to grow in full sun—that it must have some shade, as many people seem to think.

The phrase "part shade/part sun" is another confuser. This really should be: "Needs light for at least a third to half of the day. Such a plant will not thrive in full sun nor in full shade." But that is just too long to go on any tag. It may also mean to keep the plant with this requirement out of the sun during the hottest part of the day. Ask if you aren't sure. Many rhododendrons don't grow well in the hottest, sunniest positions of your garden, so they would want morning or late evening sun, which is the cool sun.

A plant labeled as needing shade needs protection from the full power of the sun all day. There are various degrees of shade, such as dappled shade (think of the spangled light beneath a wide small-leaved tree), bright shade (lots of reflected light but no light directly from the sun), light shade (similar to bright shade but a bit darker), or deep shade (dark, mysterious, and cool, with no rays of light reaching very far into this area). The deeper the shade, the less chance there is of a shade-tolerant plant producing an abundance of flowers. Ask if you're not sure.

Drought tolerance

The terms *drought resistant* and *drought loving* usually mean a plant evolved in dry areas of natural low rainfall, whether hot or not. These areas might be deserts or under big thirsty trees with a rain-shedding canopy. The term *drought tolerant* means the plant will survive occasional droughty conditions or areas that are artificially dry like sandy well-drained soils under the eaves of a building or gardens at weekend cabins in sunny areas where we are not able to water during dry or hot periods.

Once established, such plants will thrive with little or no water, but first you must establish the plant, which means making sure it doesn't completely dry out for the first two or three years in the ground. You can overwater these plants, so be careful. They need deep soakings at lengthy time intervals, depending on your summer rains and their duration, of course. Deep soakings mean that you need to run a drip system or soaker hose for three to five hours every five to ten days during dry or low rainfall periods (sometimes what seems like a rainy day is just a dust settler—no water really penetrates the soil). After one application of a soaking, dig down in the soil a foot and see how far the water went. Two feet or more of water penetration is best for shrubs and trees.

If you live in a dry-summer, wet-winter area—typically called a Mediterranean climate—your natural flora has evolved to be drought tolerant during the dry season. If you create a garden of nonnatives that require summer water around existing native plants, especially trees and shrubs, you will often have dead native plants. They cannot tolerate excessive water around their roots in the normally dry summers they evolved in. In the Puget Sound area of Washington state, many beautiful madrone trees are killed within a few weeks when home gardeners turn on the garden irrigation. I learned this lesson with the native dogwood, *Cornus nutallii*, after one summer of irrigating around a half dozen existing young trees. They were dead by autumn, to my horror. Learn the typical dates of the rainy season in your area and either use plants that only need moisture during this rainy season or don't use native plants unless they are proven to tolerate water during their normal dry season.

Hardiness

Plant tags and catalog descriptions almost always include USDA hardiness zones, but these ratings don't tell the full story. A plant labeled as tolerating temperatures of –10 degrees F in a sunny area may expire at that temperature in a shady area. Heat is often needed to toughen up a plant so it doesn't have succulent, freeze-susceptible growth going into winter. Think of a succulent, crisp head of lettuce removed from the refrigerator crisper versus one removed from the freezer after two days of freezing. The latter looks fine—until it thaws. It's the same with living plants.

Very cold-tolerant plants from lower latitudes may die during similar temperatures when in higher-latitude gardens. This happens because of the difference in the speed of change in day length as the autumn sun goes lower on the horizon; the day length changes faster closer to the poles. For example, the famous Canandaigua peaches are listed as "hardy to –25 degrees F"; in south-central Alaska where I lived, the temperatures rarely get that low for any long period, but the Canandaigua "hardy" peaches were dead right after the first light autumn frost in September because the plant's hormones did not respond to the rapidly diminishing light levels by ridding the plant of excess water in its stems as quickly as the daylight changed. The still-succulent stems burst at the first frost, just like a tightly capped bottle of water left out overnight in freezing temperatures.

The word *hardiness* should refer the amount of cold or heat a plant can tolerate, but I find that most people take the term to mean "easy to grow in my garden." When you see that term, seek clarification of what is meant. A marigold is a hardy plant—easy to grow—but it is not hardy when it comes to freezing temperatures.

Nursery or Grower Name

The last information on a plant tag should be the name of the nursery or store from which you purchased the plant. Not all nurseries put their names on the labels. Instead they have the grower—such as Proven Winners or Monrovia—print the label with its name. While tags can be expensive to print, most medium-sized retail nurseries should be proud to put their name on the tags they make for their plants. Smaller nurseries find it cheaper to print a descriptive catalog than buy expensive printing equipment. In any case, whether you do it or the nursery does, having the nursery or grower name on the tag—which you've put in your manila envelope—will help you begin to notice if there's a pattern to success or failure of plants related to the nursery of origin.

How to Choose Healthy Plants

Okay, now you've tracked down that plant you wanted and know you can grow, so how do you tell if you are getting good quality and value? In this chapter I will go through each type of plant telling you what you should look for—or be wary of. But first I will offer some general advice about what size plant you should buy and how much you should pay for it. At the end of the chapter I will tell you how to grow your own healthy plants from seed.

What Size Plant Should You Buy?

Half the pleasure of gardening is watching a plant grow and fill out. But today we live in an impatient world. We expect what we want now, and with plants we often want them full grown or at the height we need them—no taller, no shorter. When did it happen that we forgot that plants are living things not produced on demand by machines? It is an unrealistic situation we have created and one that you as a consumer should be aware of, if you aren't already. If you need immediate height or width, perhaps a man-made structure covered with an evergreen vine or espaliered plant is a better solution. I offer that sincerely. Many problems in the garden are best solved by structures and not by plants, especially in narrow yards or shady areas beneath greedy-rooted trees.

The best size to buy a plant is small. A small or seedling tree one to four feet tall will in ten years outgrow the same tree purchased at ten feet. David has had less shock, while Goliath takes years to put out a root system to support itself and the food it produces. A smaller plant also costs less, so if it dies or is destroyed by animals or crunched by delivery trucks you've lost less money and time. Certainly a great *big* tree looks impressive right away, but the care and attention it requires for several years are enormous—not to mention the financial loss and the emotional disappointment should it die.

Another important point to consider when buying small is that many rare or even good plants are not grown by the big wholesale nurseries, which tend to stick to a very limited selection. Smaller mail-order firms specializing in specific plants may be your only source for the plant or plants you

Tree Sizes

Trees are often measured or spoken of in "caliper" sizes. This is the diameter (the width from side to side, not measurement around the trunk—circumference—as is commonly thought) of the trunk at approximately six inches above ground level. For example, a designer in the United States may specify a two-inch or a five-inch caliper size. Trees may also be specified by height. When buying a tree the most important thing to look for is not size or caliper measurement but general health and shape. As for size, the most important factor is whether it fits your needs and your budget.

want. They can only grow and sell small plants, which are easier to pack and less expensive to ship. Do you really want to pay shipping for a six-to-twelve-foot-tall tree? I don't.

Now that I've said that small is better, you certainly may find very good specimen trees ten to fifteen feet tall in your local nursery (see "Tree Sizes"). A couple of strong bodies, a truck, and an easy path to the planting hole is all that's required to get the plant home. Maybe the nursery will even deliver, for a fee, to your driveway, but don't automatically expect them to place or plant. Ask before you buy.

How Much Should You Pay?

You generally get what you pay for. Experienced garden-ers can buy an inexpensive plant and turn it into something beautiful and healthy, but if you're a new gardener you should buy the freshest plants at a fair price—neither inex-pensive nor expensive—from a reputable nursery.

How do you know a fair price? Here's a technique I have found helpful. For states and countries with set minimum hourly wages, I find a good rule of thumb is that you should expect to pay these prices:

» For a basic annual like a pansy in a four-inch (or there-abouts—nine-centimeter in the United Kingdom; see "Sizes of Plant Containers") pot, slightly less than a quarter of that hourly wage.

» For a standard perennial in a four-inch pot, about half an hour's wages.

» For a gallon (or thereabouts—four-litre in the UK) peren-nial, an hour and a quarter of the minimum wage.

» For one-gallon basic, run-of-the-mill shrubs, just over an hour and a half of minimum wage.

» For a tree of standard size (and that varies according to the plant), around a day's worth of the minimum wage.

I've used this system around the United States, in Canada, in the United Kingdom, and in parts of Europe and South Africa. The consistency is within reason.

For plants that are rare and unusual to your area, or larger than normal, the prices will be what your neighborhood or town can support. No nursery will be in business long if it charges too much or too little. People won't support the former, while a business that does the latter won't be able to pay its bills. You will on occasion find flat discounts on many annuals grown in cell packs or four-inch pots. If you buy a whole flat, the discount is equivalent to getting two or three packs or pots free. Rarely is this discount applied to unusual, more expensive annuals or perennials. Some

Sizes of Plant Containers

Just as a two-by-four piece of lumber is not really two inches by four inches in dimension nor a thirty-six-inch television screen thirty-six inches wide but instead thirty-six inches on the diagonal, so are nursery pot sizes not exactly what they are called, no matter how hard the industry tries to set a standard. Industry groups such as the American Nursery and Landscape Association, the Canadian Nursery Landscape Association, and the European Nurserystock Association do provide guidelines for pot sizes and labeling. But these are only recommendations and have no effective force, so you may find variability in pot sizes at nurseries.

In the United States, standard sizes are the four-inch pot, the quart, and the gallon. I will describe these sizes here only to illustrate the discrepancy you may find between what a pot is called and its actual measurements. Standard sizes in other countries will differ.

nurseries follow the old "cheaper by the dozen" theme, offering a small discount if you get twelve of the same kind of annual or perennial—a much rarer offer with shrubs and trees, except small bare-root ones used for hedging.

Price is not necessarily a sign of quality or lack thereof. Shop around. Look at mail-order prices, remembering they will be for smaller plants.

Characteristics of a Healthy Plant

All plants should have a healthy look to them. They are living things, so if you can tell when your pets, children, spouse, friends, or other people are looking well, you can do the same with plants. Here are the general characteristics of a healthy plant:

» The small square pots that most individual perennial or annual plants come in are called four-inch pots. I suspect the measurement is taken on the diagonal—or the measurement may simply be ignored and the pot called a "four-inch" because it's close to that size. There are usually fifteen to eighteen pots of this size in a flat (the plastic tray holding them), depending on the pot's actual size.

» Large four-inch pots are sometimes called quarts but often placed and sold in the four-inch section of a nursery.

» A gallon—also known as a large quart or a six-inch pot (go figure)—is a round or square pot that a grapefruit would nest in.

» Larger pots are listed either by gallons or by the width in inches or metric measurements, often marked on the bottom. For example, a "2" on the bottom of a pot denotes a two-gallon size, "4" denotes a four-gallon size, or "18 x 10" indicates height and width in inches.

It's pretty easy to tell when a plant is unhealthy. You want to buy plants that are vigorous and perky looking.

» perky, with no wilted foliage
» full, plump, vigorous looking (unless dormant, of course)
» free of insects or signs of active insect damage
» free of signs of active disease
» not root-bound (so the pot is not bulging at the sides)
» free of dead or dying branches (except deep inside dense evergreens, which is normal)

Now we will look in more detail at what this means for each kind of plant.

Annuals

Sold in packs of from two to six cells or separately in four-inch or larger pots (rarely smaller), annuals should look in balance with the pot. The root system should be just starting to fill around the edges of the root-ball, which of course you cannot see. Ask a nursery staff person if he or she will tip the plant out of the pot so you can see the roots. Most nurseries will do that, though for some large annuals with fragile stems, like dahlias, it may not be possible.

Roots running out of the drainage holes or growing into neighboring pots most often indicate that the plant is pot-bound. This is not always a bad thing. Ask. With some plants, like marigolds, you can score the root-ball with a knife and it will stimulate the roots to grow into the soil when you pull them out of the pot just before planting. Other plants will sulk and die if you try that or will dry out because the root-

The roots of a plant should be just to the pot's edge (middle), ready to move out into your garden's soil when planted. Avoid a plant with roots that are too overgrown and compacted (right) or that hasn't produced enough roots yet to reach the pot's edges (left).

Avoid buying an instant bouquet of flowers and instead look for an annual with lots of buds showing. Invest in the future.

bound roots simply can't organize and untangle themselves enough to grow into the surrounding soil quickly enough to gather water.

Be on the lookout for plants left too long in small pots on racks in low light. Their stems will be lanky and unbranched, most obviously floppy. This is a problem with sunflowers, tomatoes, and cosmos in particular. (If you do bring home leggy tomatoes, you can bury their stems six or more inches deep or lay them in a trench, gently bending the growing tip up and out of the ground, and they will make roots all along the stem.) Also be on the lookout for yellowing leaves. They could simply be a sign of low light levels or of the plant's being moved from the perfect climate of a greenhouse to the cruel out-of-doors, or they could be a sign of disease or improper care, especially if the leaves are dried out. A couple of yellowing leaves in the midst of many healthy ones is usually nothing to be concerned about. But it's best to ask for advice if you are unsure. Be on the lookout for fungal spotting. Any tomato plant with leaf spotting or dead gray patches on the leaves is probably infected with blight and should be avoided at all costs, no matter how inexpensive. Why bring disease home under a misguided sense of economy?

An annual covered in flowers in a small pot looks perfect, but what you want to buy is an annual with lots of buds showing or just a few flowers. More often than not, a fully flowered plant has been overfed or tricked by hormones and lights to bloom early, in some cases stunting the plant—like the asters and mums sold in the autumn in small pots for instant color. They are more prone to fungal problems and frankly just look like blobs of color most of the year, never really growing to their potential. Smaller plants adjust with more ease when exposed to the brutal, real world of our gardens after leaving the controlled, gentle world of a greenhouse. You gain nothing by buying an instant bouquet of flowers on one plant except instant, temporary color.

Perennials

Make sure the description on the tag matches the characteristics of the plant you are looking at. Sometimes, customers unlike you remove a label to read and then return it to the wrong pot. A pot with a photo of a blue flower in a flat of pots labeled as yellow flowers is suspect.

Like annuals, perennials should be balanced in size with the pot and not overly pot-bound. As with annuals, small, somewhat pot-bound perennials are less of an issue if you carefully tease apart the outside roots or if the plant is divisible. The latter gets you two or three or four for the price of one! Spring or autumn is the time when such a pot-bound plant is a good value and divisible.

Root-bound perennials won't establish well unless you score the circling roots with a knife or tease them apart to break up the root-ball.

Is the plant wobbly in the pot? That is usually not a good sign, but don't test the plant by shaking the pot as if you're making a martini. A wobbly plant could be a sign of rot at the stem base, or it could indicate that the plant has just been potted into a larger pot and has not yet filled out the soil with new roots. When in doubt, ask a staff person for an opinion or to tip the plant out of the pot for you to inspect, if practical or possible.

As with annuals, be cautious of lanky plants or those with yellowing or desiccated leaves. And check out the blossoms. You do not need a perennial that was forced by heat or extra lights or hormones to bloom early. Blooms at purchase time are not terribly important, especially from

A pot-bound plant is a good value if you can gently divide the plant into two or three or four new starts.

a reputable nursery, unless you need to choose a particular color or need to see the labeled color in real life. Small containers of nonblooming plants are less expensive and establish better if you are buying several to cover a lot of ground.

Shrubs

When you are picking out shrubs, look for specimens that look vigorous, that have a good balance between top growth and the pot, and that are not root-bound, just as with annuals and perennials. The root-ball should have good heft. If it is light, it is either dried out or root-bound. Ask. Are all the branches alive? It is perfectly normal for tightly grown or pruned plants like boxwood to have dead leaves or no leaves deep inside.

When you buy a tree, the most important thing to look for is its general health and shape. The pot size should be in proportion to the top growth. Although this specimen appears healthy and vigorous, the amount of top growth suggests that the roots are not filling the pot. A well-rooted plant would have 25 to 35 percent more top growth.

Roses are shrubs and should be treated the same. One difference is that sometimes a rosebush will produce what are known as blind canes, which have no flower buds at the tip. If you look very closely you can actually see that the tip has died out and healed over. So far, even after much research, no one is absolutely certain of the cause of this odd phenomenon, but most agree that something happened to the cells in the growing tip weeks or months earlier that killed the youngest cells. The cure, thankfully, is simple: cut back the stem to a leaf about a foot or two down as if you were cutting stems for a bouquet. Within a couple of weeks, a new, flowering shoot will be growing.

Trees

Trees come from the nursery in three forms: in a pot, bare root, or balled and burlapped (that is, with a clump of burlap-wrapped soil around their roots as dug from the ground). A tree in a pot, like annuals and perennials, should have its roots just filling the pot unless the tree has just been planted in the pot bare root. Staff can tell you or find out if either is the case. If you buy a bare-root, unpotted tree, the nursery should supply a plastic bag and some wet sawdust or papers to cover the roots (but you should always travel with large plastic bags for impulse purchases of bare-root trees or freshly dug gifts from friends). Go directly home— don't stop for lunch or at the mall, parking in a sunny parking lot—and plant your new purchase, watering it in well.

A tree should have a reasonably straight trunk and a reasonably well-balanced branch structure. Don't fuss and fret about every branch and stem. It's a living being. In five to ten years some of the branches you thought were perfect will have turned ugly or have been broken by soccer balls, raccoons, snowplows, or tipsy party guests, or pruned away by you because they were too low.

The root-ball should be heavy. If it's light, it's either dried out or root-bound. Ask. Stand back to look at the whole tree. The root-ball, whether balled and burlapped or in a pot, should be in balance with the top, not so small that the tree will tip over with ease like a person balancing on one foot. The top of the tree can be wider than the root-ball, but a very tall plant should not have tiny "feet," as it were. Nor should a small tree be overplanted in a large pot, which could cause root rot. When in doubt, ask a staff person or a friend what he or she thinks.

Houseplants

What applies to perennials, shrubs, and trees also applies to choosing a healthy houseplant. In addition, you should look closely for insects on the plant. Have a salesperson help you if you are concerned. Bringing an insect-infested or diseased plant into a house is not what you want to do.

Many houseplant leaves will be covered in a chalky or dusty residue, usually a result of hard water at the grower's or from fertilizers, dust, or even a pesticide. All new houseplants, save cactus and other dry soil lovers, should be put in the shower and given a gentle rinse with tepid to cool water; then gently wipe the leaves down with a paper towel. Forget mayonnaise or plant sprays as leaf shiners. Simple water and a wipe down is all the plant needs. Science has yet to find animals in the wild applying mayonnaise to any plant, except us when we make a BLT while camping in the mountains.

Bulbs

Most bulbs are purchased as dry bulbs, tubers, or corms in spring or autumn. They should be firm and have a heft appropriate for their size. Judge them as you would an onion or a potato, which, after all, are respectively bulbs and tubers. Purchase them as soon as they arrive at the nursery and plant them immediately. If you can't plant them immediately, keep them in a warm, dry, dark place, but just for a week or two. The crisper in your fridge is not the best place as it mimics winter cooling, stimulating the bulb to try to grow, which is not what you want, unless it's a lily.

Blue mold on a hyacinth bulb is normal. Soft spots on tulip bulbs or soft narcissus (daffodil) bulbs are not good. Dust shaking out of a bulb is not good. Mummified husks of a bulb are goners. Prepackaging makes it harder to be sure all the bulbs in a packet are alive. Feel each bulb through the plastic. A reputable nursery should be willing to cut open bags until the staffer finds the three, five, or fifteen healthy bulbs a package is labeled as having. Snowdrops (*Galanthus*) are particularly fated to have one or more dead bulbs per package.

Anemone, winter aconite (*Eranthis*), foxtail lily (*Eremurus*), fritillaria (especially the smaller bulbs), crocosmia, corydalis, and trout-lily (*Erythronium*) bulbs (I use the term here in the common, not botanical, sense) do not store well out of the ground. Within a week or two of being on the nursery shelf, most are dead or near death. Buy early. Soak anemone and winter aconite bulbs in tepid water overnight before planting. This will increase your success greatly. The others mentioned can be wrapped in moist paper towels or with some wrung-out but still-moist sphagnum moss and wrapped together in plastic overnight for needed hydration. It is often better to buy these bulbs as growing plants in pots if you cannot get to your local nursery or garden center when the bulbs first arrive. If you miss the dry bulb season, many of the autumn-planted bulbs will be available potted up in spring, easy to slip into containers or among plants in the garden.

Lily bulbs are best planted in mid-to-late autumn. They are best ordered from specialist lily nurseries that will send them at the right time—and with healthy roots. Those purchased as bulbs in nurseries should have live fleshy roots when you buy them. Those with roots dried out will still grow but not as well. However, after the second year of growth the originally rootless lily should be back to normal.

Any autumn-flowering bulbs that you find flowering in the box on the nursery shelf—for example, colchicums, autumn-flowering crocus, or cyclamen—are nothing to worry about. Just go ahead and plant the bulb immediately for next autumn's display. If you leave the sprouted flowers above ground after planting, they will often perk up and turn their true darker color as if nothing untoward had happened. It is worth the investment. If you wait until next year to try and get the bulb before it flowers on the shelf, you probably will not win the race; it may take you several years to ever do so. Buy and plant as soon as you can for next autumn's display.

If you can't get to your local nursery or garden center when bulbs arrive, or they don't look plump and fresh, you can order bulbs from mail-order companies. As with all plants, you get what you pay for. Discounted or cheap mail-order bulbs are often smaller in size or diseased—not always, but much too often. With the restriction of use or banning of many agricultural chemicals worldwide (a good thing for the environment and us), it has become more expensive to grow bulbs well and large, causing a rise in prices. But a well-chosen bulb is a good investment. Most bulb mail-order companies ship when they think it's appropriate for your climate. You can make a request that they send at a different time if you need it earlier or later. However, it is up to the mail-order nursery and its digging and shipping schedule.

Mail-order companies have a wider range of varieties available, including many rare bulbs from the small specialist nurseries. The rare bulbs are often available only in limited numbers, so order as soon as the catalog arrives or is posted online. Many catalogs are available as early as June or July, so you do need to be thinking about next year's spring while this year's is still a very fresh memory.

Growing Your Own from Seed

One way to be assured of healthy plants is to grow your own from seed. Sometimes the only way to get a particular plant or variety is to grow it from seed. Other times you just want to grow something from seed or teach a child the wonders of planting a seed and watching it grow.

Buying seed

Seeds are available in nurseries and garden centers, from the catalogs of seed companies online or by mail, and from specialist seed growers and collectors. The latter deal with heirloom seeds, wild collected seeds, or specific genera or groups (primroses, hellebores, hepaticas, bulbs, or alpines are but a few); it's a world of marvels waiting for you to find online or through plant societies or sometimes only by word of mouth from those in the know.

Commercially grown seeds come in packets date stamped for the season you are buying them in—that is, seed for use in the spring or summer of 2013 should be dated "for 2013." Instructions on the back of the packet should be easy to read and understand. Most say something like "sow six weeks before last frost" or "sow after last frost." While no one really ever knows when that time will be, there is always a general time to sow that is appropriate for your area. Ask the nursery staff what that time usually is. Catalogs and websites may have some advice on that timing, too. Your local Master Gardener organization should have or be able to recommend pamphlets or books with this information for your area.

The small specialist seed companies may offer advice, but since these companies cater to the specialist, you are expected to know when to sow and how to sow this very special seed. There are many specialist books (and societies) that can give you advice on growing unusual species.

Expect a small number of seeds in a packet (especially from specialist nurseries dealing in rare seed)—five to fifty is sufficient for most except fast-growing plants like greens (lettuces, kales, spinach, and the like). Sow according to directions on the packet, thinning out if needed. Beets, for instance, naturally produce two or more seeds per seed cluster so you always have to thin them once they sprout.

Personally, I don't believe there is much of a difference between seed bought from local nurseries or garden centers versus a seed company as long as the seed is properly dated and displayed in a coolish area out of direct sun. For rarer seed, mail-order seed companies and specialist seed lists are a much better source in terms of variety and availability.

If you don't use all the seed in a packet at once, fold up

the packet, lightly tape it shut, and store it in a ziplock plastic bag, lidded glass jar, or sealed plastic container in the refrigerator. Some seed will keep for years. When you buy a bottle of vitamins or a pair of shoes, sometimes you will find a little packet in the bottle or box to absorb moisture. Toss one of them into your seed-storage container to help keep down the humidity that can rot the seed.

Starting your seeds

To start your seeds indoors or in a greenhouse instead of directly sowing them into the ground, you will need the following paraphernalia:

containers with drainage holes
(see "Containers for Starting Seeds")

a tray as deep as the containers are tall

labels

a number two graphite pencil

an appropriate sterile planting medium (soil-less mix)

a clear covering to keep moisture in, a dark one to keep light out, or a screen to keep critters out

a dibble stick

a soil heating mat or cables
and overhead lighting (optional)

Before sowing any seed, first write the name, date of sowing, number of seeds for rarer varieties, and source on a tag that you will stick in the container. You may even develop a code system that keeps writing to a minimum. For example, 13.005 could refer to the fifth packet of seed sown in 2013. In a book or on a computer, you can list this number in numerical order with genus, species, date of sowing, number of seeds (if need be), source, date of germination, and any notes about techniques used. But if that sounds too complicated (it really isn't), just put the plant's name and date of sowing on the tag and stick it in the container.

Sow the seeds in your containers in a premixed sterile seed-starting mix, usually made of peat, vermiculite, and perlite. A trick for sowing tiny seeds that helps you avoid oversowing is to mix them with a small amount of extremely fine sand and then sow the sand and seed mixture. For seeds of perennials that need some nutrients once germinated, I fill a container two-thirds full of potting soil, add a top sixth of a soilless seed-starting mix, sow the seed, and cover the seed with seed-starting mix. The seeds germinate in the sterilized mix and then push their roots into the nutrient-

Containers for Starting Seeds

Containers for starting seeds can be purchased ready-made, or if you only need a few you can make them from yogurt cups, margarine containers and tubs, styrofoam cups, and such. Wash them well and punch several holes in the bottom for drainage.

For planting containers, you can also buy peat pots and peat pellets that come as disks and expand when soaked in water. I see no need for them as they are not reusable and cost more than reusing plastic containers. They are made to decompose in the ground as long as no part of them sticks out of the soil. However, the thin netting on the peat pellet never rots, so you are adding one more bit of plastic to the ground.

I stick with plastic or sometimes clay pots. If you use the latter, be sure to soak the pots in a bucket of water first to fully hydrate them so they don't steal water from the soil. They dry out quickly, which can be a good thing, but don't let them get too dry; otherwise, every time you water, the water will go into the sides of the pot instead of the soil.

filled soil below, which gives them an extra boost early on.

This technique also helps prevent damping-off, a fungus attack that girdles the stem of a seedling where it emerges from the soil, killing it. Usually good air circulation will prevent this problem. However, should you notice any damping-off, immediately water the pot of seeds and seedlings with a fungicide for that purpose, following the directions on the package. You may be able to save uninfected seedlings and ungerminated seed. I have saved a pot or two of precious seedlings that way. If you think damping-off may be a problem, use a fungicide prophylactically when sowing the seeds.

I use this seed-sowing technique only indoors or when sowing very fine seed in pots left outdoors. Fine seed doesn't need to be covered very deeply; just a dusting of seed-starting mix is enough. The general rule is to sow the

I stopped sterilizing and washing reused plastic containers in bleach water years ago and have not had any problems, but I sow all of my seed in pots left outside to fend for themselves. If I were sowing delicate or very rare seeds prone to damping-off, I would buy a new plastic container or rinse out an old container in a sink filled with water and a tablespoon of bleach, rinsing it afterward in clear water and letting it air dry.

You can buy seed-sowing kits consisting of a flat with no drainage holes, a set of plastic cells (three packs, four packs, or six packs just like the ones many spring annuals are sold in at nurseries and garden centers) that fits the tray, and a plastic dome to cover the whole thing. They work and can be modestly priced or rather expensive. Keep them in bright light but not direct sunlight or the temperature will become too hot inside the little greenhouse, cooking the seedlings.

seed two to three times as deep as the size of the seed, though larger seeds can tolerate a deeper planting. Some seeds need light to germinate, so you would barely cover these. Other seeds need darkness; in this case, cover the container with a dark cloth or plastic and check regularly to see if germination has occurred. But most seeds are fine with just a modest covering of the soil-less mix.

Once you have sown the seed, place the containers in a deep tray—as deep as the containers are tall—and fill the tray with water halfway to the rim of the containers. The soil mix will pull water up to the top through the holes in the bottom of the containers. When the top of the soil is moist, remove the pots from the flat and put them in another flat to drain. Watering from above risks washing the seed down the interior sides of the pots or right out of the pot, so don't do it. Some seeds germinate better with heat at the root zone. Special insulated heating mats and cables are sold that can go under a tray or in a base of sand upon which the tray is placed. Follow the instructions that come with the item you purchase for safe operation.

When a seedling emerges, in most cases the first two leaves are cotyledons, a pair of food-storing leaflike struc-tures; in monocots—grasses, lilies, palms, and the like with veins parallel in the leaves—a single leaf will emerge first. The next set of leaves to appear are the true leaves and usu-ally look like the adult leaves of the grown plant. When they appear, you can transplant the seedlings into bigger pots to grow larger before planting out. I leave bulblike seedlings in the seed pot for two or three years to increase in size, then transplant when dormant.

If you sow several seeds in one pot and need to remove each (an operation called pricking out), you can do this very gently with a dibble stick—something like a long, very nar-row concave knife, a chopstick sharpened at the narrow end, or a pencil. The long narrow point allows you to tease out one seedling and its roots from another without tearing the roots, which is a very important thing not to do. Use the larger end of the dibble stick to make a hole for the seed-ling in the larger pot and gently place the seedling and its roots in the hole to the same level and depth it was in the seedling pot. Gently press the soil toward the seedling to fill the hole. Don't press very hard. Watering the seedling in its new container is usually enough to settle the soil around the roots.

Tools and Gear You'll Need

In order to put your newly purchased plants in the ground and get them off to a good start, you'll need at least some basic tools and gear. In this chapter we consider tools for digging in the soil and pruning, as well as gear to protect just about every part of the body. There are too many tools on the market from a plethora of sources, but you can find good tools on the Internet, at your local garden center or nursery, at a good hardware store that specializes in tools, and through your gardening friends. Buy good quality tools and take care of them. You get what you pay for.

My family still uses rakes and shovels that are more than sixty years old—well cared for and used for their purpose. We don't use them as pry bars. Garage and estate sales in farm country are fine places to pick up good used tools. If you buy new and the tool comes with a lifetime guarantee, keep your receipt in a place you can find it. Demand a replacement or your money back if it breaks under normal use and care. Take notice if the tool can be returned to the merchant or if you have to dance through hoops returning it to the manufacturer; better to avoid buying a tool that requires the latter.

Long-Handled Tools

Long-handled tools—shovels, rakes, hoes, spades, and other tools with handles more than three feet long—are made to keep you from bending over too far and straining your back. I use six kinds of long-handled tools: round-end shovel, spade, spading fork, broad-bladed hoe, steel-tined rake, and leaf rake. If you're a shorter person, handles can be shortened if needed. Taller people may need to look far and wide to find a handle long enough for themselves. Don't buy short.

Handles are made from wood, metal, or fiberglass. I prefer wood because it is lighter. Be sure to buy quality; a cheap wooden-handled shovel that snaps during digging is not only frustrating and useless but also potentially dangerous. If you like fiberglass handles, buy them. There is nothing inherently wrong with them. They are stronger than most woods. The difference is really subjective.

Wooden handles are mostly made of ash—a strong, straight-grained wood. The handle should be wiped down every so often (this isn't a science, but at least twice a year—and certainly before putting away for the off season) with mineral oil or any other wood oil to keep it from drying out and cracking. If the grain raises a sharp edge, give the handle a quick rubdown with sandpaper to smooth off the potential splinters, then oil.

The metal working end of a tool—the blade, rake tines,

When you buy long-handled tools, look for a working end of 14 gauge metal or more and a shank at least a foot long affixing the working end to a sturdy handle.

and so forth—should be of 14 gauge thickness or more; otherwise the blade will fold like a sheet of thin plastic at the first hard dig or pull. It should also have a shank (the metal part of the working end that goes up and wraps around and affixes it to the handle) running at least a foot—better two—up the wooden handle, because that is where the stress is greatest. A long shank provides more support and less breakage. A tool with the metal working end just wedged into the handle with a spike and then covered over with a thin metal cap is a tool to walk away from. It will soon break where the metal is inserted into the handle, or the metal part will fall out of the handle, never again to fit properly.

The handle end of a long tool sometimes ends in a D-shaped grip made of wood, metal, or hard plastic. Make sure it fits your hand and has no sharp edges that will cut or cause blisters. If wooden, it too should be oiled regularly. The D-shaped grip should also have a shank going down the wooden shaft nine inches or so.

With all long-handled tools, it is very important to clean and dry them after each use. After cleaning, the metal working ends can be plunged in and out of sand mixed with mineral oil to prevent rust. The ratio of mineral oil to sand isn't critical, but a quart of oil to an average-sized bucket of washed sand is plenty. Slowly stir the two together with a trowel. Some gardeners worry about contaminating their ground with mineral oil, so they use vegetable oil instead. I have no experience with that but do recommend you keep the bucket covered to discourage animals from digging in it. Remake the mixture once a year.

Keep shovel, spade, and hoe blades sharpened with a simple hand rasp that has a fine set of teeth, or use a file with a slightly coarser set of teeth made for such a purpose. The blades do not have to be knife-edge sharp but should be free of burrs and bluntness. If you are puzzled about how to do this, stop by your local machine shop or hardware store and ask for some pointers on sharpening, or look online for a how-to video. Rakes don't need sharpening.

A word about ergonomic long-handled tools. These are tools with a handle bent in such a way as to take the strain off the user's back or arms. I have tried several, especially snow shovels, and not noticed any difference in how I felt afterward. I suspect this is because I'm a tall person and the tools are made for people of average height. They are good tools and they do work for many people. Try one out. Ask the store what its return policy is. If you feel better or feel no strain after using one, it's the tool for you.

If you suffer from arthritis or any other condition that impedes your strength or interferes with holding a tool, you might be interested in the many specially designed tools on the market. Type "garden tools for arthritic hands" into an Internet search engine and explore the many options.

Shovels

Shovels come in two basic shapes —round-end scoops and straight-edge flats. A round-end, the stereotypical shovel a child might draw, is used for digging and, well, shoveling. The sharp point and curved shape slice easily through soil. It should not be used to shovel soil or gravel off of concrete or asphalt surfaces as this quickly wears away the tip and erodes the usefulness of the shovel for digging. I use a round-end shovel when I have to dig out a plant with a rounded rootball, or for moving lots of soil around, or digging up big beds deeply and quickly.

A square-end flat-bottom shovel with slightly bent up sides is best for shoveling piles of soil, compost, or gravel from pile to wheelbarrow, path, or garden. It also works better for scooping up debris and soils on flat, hard surfaces. It is nearly useless for digging. I rarely use a flat-bottomed shovel except for moving soil or mulches around if no other shovel is available.

Keep the edges sharp on either of these shovels so they work efficiently.

Spades

Spades look like shovels but have a flat blade with a straight, sharp end. They pierce the soil easily, make clean edges, and are useful for slicing straight down into the soil. I use them to edge beds and to dig out plants when I need to cut straight down alongside, not under, the plant. A spade is good for turning over soil in a bed and also for stripping sod when you want to turn a patch of lawn into a path or bed. I use a spade more than a shovel when digging in the garden. It's just a personal preference.

Spades come with short or long handles. Use whichever fits your height and saves you from an aching back. Surprisingly, a short-handled one often works well for tall people, as I can attest from personal experience.

Spading forks

Unlike a pitchfork, which has long, thin, rounded tines that curve upward to form a slight scoop, a spading fork (also called a garden, digging, or border fork) has four broad, flat tines that project in a flat plane. The tine area is about the same size as a spade blade. A spading fork is excellent for breaking up compacted ground, digging out plants where

Round-end shovels are best for digging and moving lots of soil around, while square-end shovels are best for scooping up soil or gravel from a flat, hard surface. Spades are great for edging beds and stripping sod.

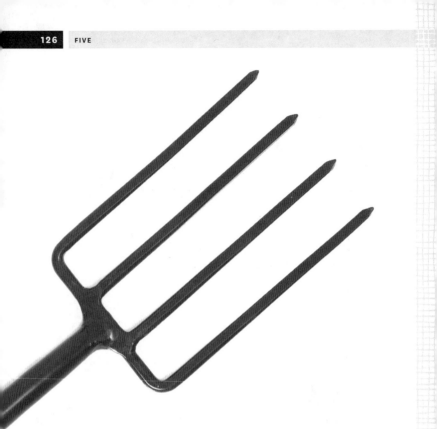

Spading forks are useful for breaking up hard soil, digging out plants, and chucking compost into a bed.

you don't want to sever many roots, and chucking and fluffing manure or compost into a bed. I wouldn't be without one.

Spading forks, like spades, usually come with a shorter handle but can be found with long ones for taller people. Try either to see which best fits your height and your ability to bend and lift the weight at the end of the fork.

Hoes

Hoes come with broad blades either long or short in depth, narrow blades, and heart-shaped blades. There is also the scuffle hoe (also known as a hula or stirrup hoe), which looks like a saddle stirrup. Each has a specific purpose, but most home gardeners need only one, maybe two at the most: a scuffle hoe and a standard broad-bladed hoe.

The standard broad-bladed hoe is used to chop out bigger weeds and create a shallow or deep furrow. The crook where the blade meets the metal shaft connecting it to the handle is made to be bent. Do not leave it at the angle it was at purchase. Position the handle so it is at a comfortable angle for you, ignoring the angle of the blade, then bend the crook above the blade so that the blade lies parallel to the ground. With a simple gliding motion over the ground you can cut off weeds at their base. You can also use it to chop through fine roots, scoop up a bit of soil, and cultivate the top couple of inches of soil.

The narrow-bladed hoe is just a lighter version of the broad-bladed one. It is best used for light hoeing of weed seedlings, since it doesn't have enough heft to do any chopping. The hoe with a heart-shaped blade is usually used to dig small furrows or trenches for planting seeds or seedlings. Its narrow point it also very helpful in teasing out weeds in tight places and scooping out a bit of soil to make a small planting hole. Treat and adjust it as you would the other hoes.

The scuffle hoe is ideal for shallow weeding of annual weed seedlings. You simply move the hoe back and forth lightly over the ground about a quarter inch below the soil surface, slicing off the weeds below the crown. By using the same technique, you can also create a dust mulch surface

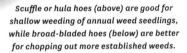

*Scuffle or hula hoes (above) are good for
shallow weeding of annual weed seedlings,
while broad-bladed hoes (below) are better
for chopping out more established weeds.*

in dry soils that is inhospitable to most annual weed seeds germinating.

Rakes

There are two basic kinds of rakes: broad rakes with rigid steel tines curved down, and fan-shaped leaf rakes with flexible tines.

Broad steel-tined rakes are ideal for moving soil around to create a planting area. Use the rake with the tines downward to move large amounts of soil. Turn it over and use the flat backside to smooth out the planting area with finesse. This kind of rake is also good for raking out roots, rocks, and clods of soil from the top of a newly dug bed. I have used it to hand thatch a lawn, pulling the old dead grass out of the sod and opening up the turf for fertilizer and water. There are thatching machines for this work, but sometimes it's easier to use a steel-tined rake.

Broad rakes with long tines can be made of wood or bamboo and are used for raking loose soil into small furrows,

Broad rakes with rigid steel tines are useful for moving heavy loose materials like soil, sand, and gravel.

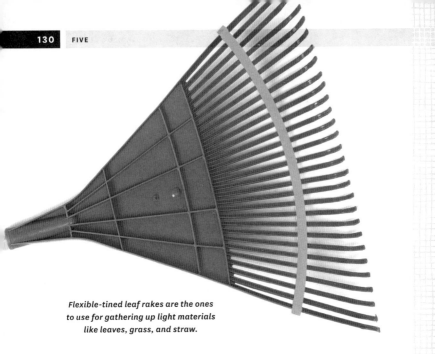

Flexible-tined leaf rakes are the ones to use for gathering up light materials like leaves, grass, and straw.

raking up small twigs and leaves, and making the regular-spaced sinuous rows in Zen gravel gardens.

For raking up leaves, nothing works better than the fan-shaped leaf rake. Whether made of steel, aluminum, plastic, or bamboo, this kind of rake works best with a light touch. Do not use with a heavy hand. You'll just end up gouging leaves and clods of dirt out of the ground. Rake with a light, delicate pressure in short strokes toward your body. Think of the light, soothing touch you would use in petting a dog or a cat. Bamboo lawn rakes wear out quickly with a heavy hand. I do not particularly like the plastic ones, finding them too stiff, the tines lacking the spring of the metal ones, which I find necessary to fluff the leaves out of grass or around corners.

Short-Handled Tools

Short-handled tools—to use while sitting or kneeling—include trowels, hand forks, weeding knives, and bulb

Trowels are useful for planting small starts and bulbs. Hand forks are good for roughing up soil in tight places.

planters. Don't buy inexpensive hand tools made of thin metal. They are just not worth the money, being too easy to bend and often having sharp edges on handles or unwelded seams that cut hands or let in water and moisture, allowing a wooden handle to rot. I look for stainless steel working parts with all seams and joints welded and ground smooth, and strong-shaped handles for good gripping. I expect a well-made tool, with proper care, to outlast me. So should you.

Trowels

Trowels are the little hand shovels that come in a bewildering range of shapes and sizes. I prefer two, both with wooden handles: a long and wide trowel and a long and narrow one, both with concave blades. The latter is sometimes called a bulb planting trowel as the blade is narrow enough to make a hole in the ground the size of most bulbs. Ignore the other kinds of trowels unless your type of gardening or hand needs one of those specialty trowels.

Trowels are good for planting small transplants like annuals grown in four-inch pots or cell packs, for digging up small seedlings, and for planting bulbs. Hold the trowel like a dagger with the handle facing down and stab it into the soil, pulling toward you when the blade is in the ground. This usually makes a V- or U-shaped hole of sufficient size to put a small plant or bulb in.

Hand forks

Hand forks, also known as claw forks, are usually three tined. These are used to rough up or open up soil in tight places such as around clumps of perennials where a hoe would be too big. This is how I use them, but rarely. Other people use them regularly.

Weeding knives

Many pro and amateur gardeners I know use a weeding knife known as a hori-hori (or as a farmer's weeder or Japanese trowel) as their basic hand tool. The hori-hori comes from Japan and was made to dig out mountain trees and shrubs to be used as bonsai. It looks like a straight, thick dagger twelve to fifteen inches long with a wooden handle taking up about half or slightly less than half of the length. The blade is slightly concave and sharply serrated on one edge, and sharp and smooth like a knife on the other. Along the edges are marks indicating inches or centimeters, useful for measuring depth or spacing when planting.

This is one of the tools newer to Western culture and deservedly very popular. It digs out weeds with taproots like dandelions, cuts through many shrub and tree roots, and can be used as a saw and a measuring device. This is one of the few tools I've mentioned that can be used to pry things out of the ground. All the other tools are apt to break if used with a lot of pressure as you would use a pry bar. (But if you have stony soil that requires prying out of rocks, by all means buy a heavy-duty long steel pry bar.)

Bulb planters

Bulb planters are tapered metal tools looking like a piece of pipe with a wooden handle across the wide end and measured markings on the sides.

A weeding knife or hori-hori can be used to dig out taprooted weeds like dandelions, cut through roots, saw, and measure.

Plunge the planter into the ground to the desired depth marked on the outside, twist slightly, then pull out, taking a plug of soil with you. Drop in the bulb, turn over the planter, and knock the plug of soil out and into the hole. While most bulb planters are hand held, some are at the end of a long rod with a T-handle at the top and a flange at the base for your foot, all to save stooping. Use your foot to plunge the planter into the ground, and repeat the same actions used with the hand-held one. These are useful in soft soils but not practical in rooty, dense, or rocky soils. I find I can plant much faster with a trowel—and a decent wrist brace!

Pruning Tools

You will need pruning tools—hand pruners, loppers, and pruning saws—to keep your shrubs and trees shapely and well proportioned as they grow. As with planting tools, look for solidly constructed tools and keep them clean, oiled, and sharpened. Don't skimp on cost. A good tool is a good investment. You will also find a smallish plastic tarp—six by six feet or ten by ten feet—useful for hauling away pruned twigs and branches.

Hand pruners

Hand pruners, known as secateurs in the United Kingdom and French-speaking countries, are useful for cutting the dead flowers off perennials (deadheading) and snipping small twigs. Never use a pair of hand pruners on branches or sticks larger than a half inch in diameter. While your own strength may make the pruners cut through the branch, you risk twisting the blades out of alignment. For these larger branches, use loppers.

Hand pruners should fit your hand and are useful for deadheading and snipping twigs. Loppers are better suited to removing and cutting up branches up to two inches in diameter.

Invest in a good pair of hand pruners that have blades that pass by each other like a pair of scissors, not a pair where the top blade presses down on the bottom one like a hammer on an anvil. You get a cleaner cut with bypass pruners. This is where spending money will serve you well in the long run. A pair of hand pruners that can be easily dismantled, cleaned, and sharpened, and with parts that can easily be replaced, is the kind to look for.

Pruners come in various sizes and shapes for small, medium, and large hands, and for right- or left-handed people. Some have a handle that rotates as you squeeze the handles together, giving extra leverage to not-so-strong hands. Test a few. Your pruners should feel right for your hand—not too small or too big.

Keep your pruners clean, oiled, and sharpened. If you do not know how to sharpen pruners to a beveled edge, take them to a professional. Usually a professional knife sharpener can do the job. Do not use an electric kitchen knife sharpener on your pruners!

It is a good idea to buy a leather holder to attach to your belt to carry your pruners. This limits putting a hole in your back pocket or falling backward onto the pruners and putting a hole in yourself.

Loppers

Loppers are simply long-handled pruners used to remove small limbs from trees, cut up limbs into smaller pieces for hauling away, and reach into thorny shrubs from a safe distance. Again, I recommend a bypass model. Most will cut through branches up to two inches in diameter before you risk twisting the blades out of alignment. I no longer buy pruning loppers with wooden handles unless they are extremely well made. I prefer sturdy metal or fiberglass handles that won't bend or break. Some come with extendable, telescoping handles. Make sure the screw latch locking the extended handles is sturdy and easy to use and won't come loose during use.

Pruning saws

Pruning saws are used for cutting larger limbs—anything more than about two inches in diameter—from trees and for cutting larger limbs into smaller pieces to haul away. They come with blades that are either rigidly attached to the handle or that can be folded back into the handle. The choice is a matter of personal preference, though those that fold back are easier to carry around. Pruning saws of any type should have large teeth with largish spaces between the teeth. Small teeth clog up too easily, especially when cutting through sappy trees like pines or firs. The blade of a pruning saw is slightly arched, not straight like a carpenter's saw, forcing the blade into the cut as you pull back and giving extra strength and stability to your backstroke.

For pruning high up in a tree, there are extendable pole saws with the blade at the tip. It's important to wear protective eye gear when using any pruning saws, to keep the sawdust from falling into your eyes while you look up to make sure it's the limb and not some cable you are sawing away at. Use caution when cutting something above you. You don't want a large limb falling on your head or the neighbor's car. If a branch is too big for you to handle, call a professional arborist. They are much cheaper than doctor or hospital visits.

Look for a pruning saw that is sturdy, well made, and easy to maintain, and pass up anything gimmicky. Most

Pruning saws can have rigid or collapsible blades but are the tool of choice for cutting limbs more than about two inches in diameter.

companies that make good shovels, spades, pruners, or rakes also make good pruning saws. Buy a good quality one and have it professionally sharpened. Wipe the blades and handles clean after each use. You can clean off any pitch or sap by pouring boiling water over the blade and then wiping it off with a rag while the pitch is still soft. Dry thoroughly afterward to prevent rusting. Mineral spirits, too, will soften any pitch so that you can wipe it off.

Protective Gear for Safe Gardening

Now we'll discuss the protective gear you'll need when you venture into the garden to plant and prune. For those of you under thirty who think you can skip this section, I offer this morality tale. When I was in my early twenties, I worked at a nursery owned by my late grandfather's best friend, Virgil Eckert. He was then in his eighties. Each day we'd dig the next day's orders of trees and shrubs. He would watch me digging a tree, on my knees, twisting and turning and wrestling to get the root-strong plant out of the ground. "Jim," he said one day as he stood leaning on his much-needed cane, "Don't do what I did. Take care of your body while you're young. You know, you'll have plenty of time to injure it when you get older." Thirty or so years later, I know what he means: gardening need not be a contact sport. Now read on, please.

Hands and arms

Gloves are as much a necessity as a fashion statement. The variety of gloves available on the market makes Mrs. Marcos's famed shoe collection look paltry. How do you choose? Simple: practicality.

To my mind, gloves come in two types: those that keep your hands clean yet provide dexterity and preserve the sense of touch, and those that protect your hands—and arms—from injury by thorn, needle, and caustic saps. Of the first, there are disposable gloves, thin washable cloth gloves, and woven cloth gloves with rubber- or plastic-coated palms and fingertips (also washable). Some are form-fitting elastic, some printed with cute patterns or sayings, others just cloth and rubber or vinyl coated. The only gloves that protect your hands from most garden injuries are thick leather gloves. Regardless of the type, buy a size that fits well, neither too snug nor too loose, which can cause blisters.

I like to be able to feel my way around the soil, the crown of a weed when pulling it out, and little bulbs in the soil as I muck around, so most often I use disposable, nonlatex surgical gloves. They keep my hands clean—when they don't tear—and let me retain my sense of touch. I can go through several in a project as some varieties tear more easily than others, but the ability to retain the sense of touch is important.

Thin cloth gloves with no plastic or rubber are the next level of glove protection. They are good for dry days in the garden. In rain or wet they are like a sponge and soon become soggy and cold, highly capable of creating blisters. They are washable.

The next step up are the woven cloth gloves with the palms and finger bottoms and tips covered in rubber or soft plastic, like a movie star's hands after making prints in wet cement in front of Grauman's Chinese Theater. Inexpensive, they provide modest protection from water, can be washed, and last for months, depending on how much hard work you do. The fingertips usually wear out first. When washing and drying, I turn them inside out before putting them in the dryer—don't worry if the fingers just ball up in the glove—and dry on a cooler temperature so I don't risk melting the plastic covering. For ultimate safety, turn inside out and hang to air dry.

Leather gloves are best for pruning roses and other thorny plants, or hauling lots of brush. Those that extend up the arm provide protection when you reach deep into thorny thickets and aren't wearing long sleeves. It's important to clean and dry these gloves after each use. If recommended by the manufacturer, saddle soap or similar leather treatment can be used to keep them soft and supple. Nothing is harder on your hands than hard, dry gloves. Leather gloves are expensive but a good investment if well cared for.

If you think you need the plastic arm guards sometimes offered in garden supply catalogs, you really should be calling in an expert pruner or arborist—or you are one.

Elbows, wrists, legs, and knees

Knees need the most protection. As children we can crawl about on our knees on almost any surface and never get a scratch or blemish or feel creaky. I wish I could retain the knees I had at five years old until I expire at a very advanced age. Getting on your knees in the garden is the best way to save your back, keep your lunch in your stomach, keep from passing out and taking a tumble from bending over too far, or get a good close view of what it is you are weeding or planting.

I solve the problem by sitting in a side-saddle position on the ground, rarely on my knees. But if I were to weed and kneel in the garden I'd get a very good, well-cushioned pair of knee pads that firmly remain attached to my legs at the knees. Each of us is built differently, so go to a garden or hardware store to try a pair, taking a test kneel on the concrete floor. Don't be falsely humble or embarrassed. If they don't feel comfortable on the store's concrete floor, they won't in the garden. If you are buying by mail order or through the Internet, make sure you can return them after

Kneeling pads with or without handles can save your knees in the garden.

testing them on a thinly carpeted floor. Surprisingly, or perhaps not, the building industry has some of the best. Others are sold at garden shows. Ask your friends. One pre–Baby Boomer friend of mine who gardens in Alaska says, "Real gardeners don't use knee pads! . . . They get their knees good and muddy and bruised from the occasional rock and when it gets to be too much, they come in for hot tea and aspirin." She uses "an old beach towel folded many times as a kneeling pad [only] when the ground is still cold." She adds, "I consider kneeling in the grass a penance for having the temerity to think that I can make things grow." Now that's a humble gardener—because she *can* make things grow.

Kneeling pads, rectangles of soft foam or rubber about a foot by two feet, work better than folded towels, I think, but I'm not as humble as my friend. The plants should bear some of the blame. I use a piece of styrofoam or a couple of layers of cardboard or made-for-the-garden knee pads. There are kneeling pads made with metal handles a foot or more tall rising up from each end that you can grasp at the top to help push yourself back upright. If you get one of these, just make sure it is well made, strong, and high enough to fit you. Don't be tempted to turn a handled pad over to use as a stool or you're sure to go head first into the border, with no handles to ease your bruised ego back up, never mind the bruised plants. As with all tools, try them out in the store first.

As for elbows, these are most often hurt from repetitive motion, not by banging into rocks and walls (although a simple pair of elbow pads will protect you there). Tennis elbow is the most common elbow injury from gardening and the one most simply fixed. You can buy cuff straps made for tennis elbow injuries at a drugstore in the wrist and arch support section. They snuggly wrap around your forearm two to three inches below the elbow. Use them whenever working in the garden or writing up your notes (finger movement is one of the worst triggers of tennis elbow pain). Consult your doctor about taking an anti-inflammatory drug. I cured my own tennis elbow within a few weeks and keep it away by using cuff straps every so often.

Regarding wrists, if you are prone to or have carpel tunnel syndrome, use wrist braces and follow your doctor's advice about hot or cold packs and anti-inflammatories.

As for your legs, shin guards are usually not needed unless you have a habit of banging your shinny shin shins into things.

Eyes and ears

Being aware of the lurking dangers to your eyes and ears is your best protection. When working in shrubs, you could push sideways into a shrub and have a twig go in your ear. If this worries you, use simple foam earplugs. When you use power tools, a good set of ear pads/mufflers is essential to protect your ears from damaging noise.

Eyes are trickier. A pair of glasses if you wear them, or a pair of plain glass glasses if you don't, work fairly well, but plastic goggles provide all-round protection. I used to think they were a bit extreme, but the more I work around thin-twigged shrubs, the more wary I am of twig tips poking my eyes or bits of sawdust scratching my corneas and rattling my nerves. When you use saws—power or hand—goggles are a smart idea.

Head

A hat or scarf gives excellent protection from sunburn or rain. A hat should have a wide brim. Baseball caps cover the top of a head and shade the eyes but do nothing for ears, napes of necks, and sides of faces, where many gardeners get their first carcinomas. I like a straw hat or one made of some other woven plant material because both let the head breathe and the heat out. I'm a hothead when I work, so wearing a nonbreathing hat is torture. There are hats with a flap of material hanging from the back—like a French Foreign Legion desert-issue hat—to protect your neck. You can also tuck a towel under your hat and let it drape over your nape.

Some clothes are now made with built-in sun protection rated on a UPF (ultraviolet protection factor) scale that considers both UVA and UVB (if you want more info on these, check the Web or ask your doctor). A UPF rating of 50+ is the highest you need and the highest standard recommended. Paying for a higher number is a waste. I have not used this type of clothing, but it is a good idea. Most outdoor recreation stores sell such clothes.

Whatever you wear, use a good sunscreen too. Sunscreens are a must on sunny or bright days, and a waterproof (sweatproof, really) variety is best. Many of us don't want to wear long-sleeved clothing because of the heat buildup. All sunscreens block UVB rays; some block UVA rays. According to new rules from the U.S. Food and Drug Administration that took effect in the summer of 2012, if a sunscreen is labeled as "broad spectrum," it blocks both. The SPF (sun protection factor) rating of a sunscreen refers to how long you can stay out in the sun before burning. On products without the broad-spectrum claim, SPF rates only UVB protection. On broad-spectrum sunscreens, higher SPF numbers mean more protection against UVB as well as more protection against UVA. SPF 15 means you can stay out fifteen times longer than it normally takes you to burn. A rating beyond SPF 40 is useless because during that period of time the sunscreen will probably have worn or been wiped off. It's important to understand that SPF and UPF rating numbers do not correlate.

See your doctor regularly to be checked for any questionable spots on your skin, especially your head, arms, and shoulders.

Feet

Wear good sturdy footwear: it's as simple as that. If your feet ache after being out in the garden, check your arch supports and the length of your legs (some of us were not born with legs made to match). If you have weak ankles, wear boots that lace up over your ankles for sturdy support.

I used to wear real wooden Swedish clogs when I gardened, just like my ancestors. Historically correct they were, but stone, dirt, and water collectors they were too. Wear what's appropriate for you and your feet, but certainly with a sturdy hard sole, especially for bashing the bottom of your foot against a shovel when digging.

Miscellaneous protection

For those who garden "in the altogether"—and I don't mean with a group of friends—just be very careful and use lots of sunscreen and mosquito repellent. Have solid high fences or hedges to protect the delicate sensibilities of your neighbors. And beware of your own delicate sensibilities, especially if dogs with cold noses are prone to visit you.

I know there are a lot of you behind those fences and hedges. After all, the original residents of Eden gardened in the altogether, but unlike them, most gardeners can't grow figs in their climates.

How to Establish Your New Plants

Coming home with a load of new plants can be exhilarating as you imagine future years of cutting flowers, sitting under the shade of your new tree, or eating fresh homegrown vegetables. But practical matters come first—your purchases need to be properly placed and planted. If the plants came right out of a greenhouse, they will need hardening off for a few days. Put them in a lightly shaded area and water them well for two or three days. Then move them into a lighter area for another two or three days, after which you can plant them out into their proper spots.

The Best Time to Plant

There was a time not so long ago when plants were not sold in containers. Up to the middle of the twentieth century—and even into the era of the Flower Child—plants were dug from the ground when dormant, wrapped in wet newspapers, waxed paper, wood shavings, or burlap bags, and sent off to the gardener, to be planted as soon as they arrived. Selling and buying of plants throughout the year was uncommon, if not unheard of. Things have changed. Today's customer expects a plant in season or even year-round.

But now that we can buy most plants anytime the weather and season allow, we must remember that this convenience comes at a price. One price is that plants in containers can quickly become root-bound, needing our help to become unbound and established. Besides, this relatively new way of growing and buying plants in containers confuses people when it comes to the proper time to plant. Even though plants are available for a much longer selling time, many people still think that only spring or autumn is an appropriate planting time, and that you won't have to water if you plant in the latter season. Unfortunately, some garden writers and publishers add to this confusion by repeating advice and instructions from more than sixty years ago when plants were purchased bare root.

The correct answer to "When is the best time to plant?" is this: when you have the plant in hand and can dig in the ground. In Alaska I planted lilies in early November, having dug the hole earlier and covered it with boards, straw, and a tarp to keep the soil unfrozen until the bulbs arrived. In Washington I have planted every month of the year whenever a shovel can penetrate the soil—that is, whenever the ground is not frozen or a sodden shovel-gripping muck.

People fret, "What do I do with the plant until I can plant it?" If it is in a pot, just keep it in the pot and watered, just like a nursery would. Bonsai plants remain in pots for centuries—specially treated, of course—so spending a few weeks or months in a pot, kept watered and in the proper light, will be fine for any potted plant.

Transplant is a very confusing word to the new gardener, almost as confusing as *hardy*. The word means to dig from the ground and move to another location. This involves severing much of the plant's root system, thereby injuring the plant by reducing its food supply and its ability to take up water and nutrients. It is best done when the plant is dormant. The word does not mean removing a plant from a pot and planting it in the ground, which causes minimal injury and can be done at any time the ground is ready.

Proper Siting

If you have done your homework, read the tag, or listened to a successful gardener, you will have chosen the right location for the plant or the right plant for the situation. Unless you garden to experiment, don't force a plant to grow somewhere it cannot.

Be mindful of power lines and eaves and the *ultimate* height of anything you plant beneath them. You don't want to be pruning off the top of a tree once or twice yearly.

Planting many trees—especially those with grand constitutions—in a lawn can eventually kill the grass beneath if the limbs are low. Consider if that's what you want to have happen. Will their greedy roots push up sidewalks, push in basement walls, or ruin your cobbled driveway? Or will they remain decently deep below ground? As mentioned earlier in the book, try not to plant over sewer lines so as not to bung them up or lose the tree if the lines have to be dug up and replaced.

Leave room between plants or garden beds and walls or fences so painters can do their job without having to tiptoe around your tulips or tiarellas. Think ahead about any potential repairs, house expansions, problems, or limits of the potential site versus the needs, greeds, and deeds of the plants nearby.

Many a broadleaf evergreen or semi-hardy plant needs protection from early morning and midday sun during freezing weather. The frozen leaves and stems can burst and die when the morning sun hits them. We used to think this happened because the morning sun heated the plant tissues too fast, causing the water within to boil. Not so, now say the scientists, but they don't really know what it is that does happen, just that it happens. If you have a plant that will get this sun exposure, here's a simple technique to protect it in winter. Place a loose layer or two of a spun fabric agricultural row cover, pinned against winds, over the plant. This provides sufficient protection in mild winter areas and in some harsher ones to slow or halt the thawing process. Burlap or hessian (which provides the best protection of all) is useful, especially in severe winter areas, but may be too heavy, especially in a winter rain or in heavy snow. Never, ever use plastic. It heats up, holds in moisture, and acts like a small greenhouse, creating the very conditions you are trying to prevent.

If you have standing water in your garden, consult a professional about ways to get the water out and away in a safe and practical manner. Standing water, unless turned into a pond, is not a place to be gardening. Nor do you want to simply direct it toward your neighbor's or the street—unless you like sitting in courtrooms and paying attorneys.

Planting Annuals and Perennials

To prepare a bed for annuals or perennials, I put a thick layer of a feeding mulch over the area. (Feeding mulches release nutrients into the soil and include compost and rotted manures mixed with decomposed wood products such as bark, sawdust, or wood chips. More on feeding mulches in chapter 7.) Then as I dig in each plant, I'm mixing this feeding mulch with the native soil. Much easier than doubling digging (see "Is Double Digging Necessary?").

Dig a hole wide and deep enough to accommodate the root-ball or bare roots, spreading out the roots in either case. With a pot-bound plant, you may have to cut or tear away some of the tightly bound roots, loosening the root-ball so the root ends are surrounded by soil. Place the plant in the ground so that the point where the roots meet the stem or stems is level with the ground's surface. Backfill with soil dug out from the hole, gently firm the soil around the plant—not too hard (as many authors tell us to do) or you risk compacting the soil—and then water to settle the soil around the plant. If pockets open up or the soil settles below the root-ball, add more of the excavated soil and water in. When finished with all the planting—if you have not previously mulched—place a two- or three-inch layer of feeding mulch over the whole bed for enrichment and to cover any weed seeds you brought to the surface during digging.

Most vines you buy will be bare at the base, which is not a problem. Clematis should have its root-ball planted about three to four inches below the ground level; bury the stem and then cut back the growth above ground to one foot to make it branch well. It sounds terrible, but it's best for the plant as it forces the clematis to form more roots on the stems and also protects susceptible varieties from clematis wilt. Cutting back forces more stems to develop, making a bushier plant and making it easier to cut back a few stems in stages over a couple of years instead of all at once to rejuvenate the vine.

Planting Bulbs

Unless planting instructions sent with the bulbs say otherwise, most bulbs do well planted at a depth three times the height of the bulb. For example, a daffodil bulb three inches high should be placed in the bottom of a hole nine inches deep; a one-inch-high bulb should be planted three inches deep. The top should be pointing up. If you don't know which end is the top, you can always plant a bulb on its side, and in time it will right itself. If you use manures or soils containing manures, place two or more inches of manure-free soil on top of this layer and then over the bulb to avoid getting manure on the bulb when planting, which may encourage rotting.

Is Double Digging Necessary?

Double digging used to be recommended when creating a border or large planting bed. The term means digging to a depth two spade or shovel blade lengths into the soil and doing all sorts of mixing of old and new soils, and other labor-intensive things. It's a technique picked up and bandied about by lecturers and writers in other countries to sound very much the proper gardener. But, thank goodness, it is not necessary.

First off, it's a lot of work—unneeded in my opinion and experience—that creates too many aches and pains for the gardener. Second, in clay soils it creates a nondraining pit/pot/sump that will be nothing but trouble—unless you provide drainage out of this pit. Third, and most important, it—along with rototilling, a very American thing to do—destroys the structure of your native soil. In this era of concern for the environment and for maintaining healthy soils, it's time to say that double digging is not a good thing.

Planting Shrubs and Trees

For large shrubs and trees, dig a hole no deeper than the height of the root-ball but at least three times wider. As you dig, set the soil to one side on a plastic tarp. Fill the hole up with water. If it empties in less than thirty minutes, fill it up one or two more times to get the ground beneath the root-ball good and moist so that the roots will work their way down, creating a more drought-resistant plant. If it takes more than thirty minutes to drain, your soil is clayey and this one-time below watering, as I call it, is enough. If it takes longer than an hour, this is probably not the right place to be planting a tree or shrub unless it loves ponds and swamps.

Remove the tree or shrub from the pot. If you see roots circling around the edges of the root-ball, be ruthless and cut them off; chop at them with a machete if needed, going in

As I don't believe gardening should be a contact sport, I recommend that all gardeners, especially beginning gardeners, choose plants suited to your native soil and avoid all this digging business. If you need to improve, open, or increase the organic matter in your soils, do what nature does and annually mulch the surface of the soil with a feeding mulch containing lots of compost, well-rotted manures, and the like. In time worms and seasonal freezing and thawing will work it all down into the soil. (You can take a spading fork and tease the two layers together, but nothing too demanding is needed.) I've seen it happen in my own garden in just two years. Gray, sticky clay became friable, humus-infused soil with just two annual mulchings and letting the worms have a go at it. Rather miraculous—and clever on my part, I thought at the time. But I was inspired by reading garden books by Graham Stuart Thomas and Beth Chatto—two people much ahead of the times and whose books I recommend.

When there are circling roots, remove the entire outer inch of the sides and bottom of the root-ball before planting a tree or shrub.

about an inch or two deep so there are no circling roots left.

Place the plant in the center of the hole, keeping the top of the root-ball as close to the level of the soil as possible. Backfill with the soil you took out. Do not amend the soil with compost or anything else. Amending the soil should no longer be recommended by gardeners, horticulturalists, or nurseries, especially if they've paid attention to several studies of thirty and forty years duration that concluded that amending just the planting hole will encourage the plant's roots to stay within the hole and not spread out properly beyond it. If a tree or shrub cannot grow in the existing soil of your garden, you have purchased the wrong plant.

If your tree comes with its root-ball wrapped in burlap, place the wrapped root-ball in the hole before removing the burlap. Sometimes the soil is loose and will fall away if you unwrap it at this point. If you have it at the right level, then cut away the string, fold back the burlap, and remove it as gently as possible either by rolling it out from under the plant or cutting it away. Then scratch around the sides of the root-ball with a hand fork to loosen the soil a bit and look for any damaged roots. Also remove any soil at the top burying the stem. Some professionals recommend removing all the soil from such plants at this time. This is acceptable if and only if the plant is dormant, so unless you know what you are doing—don't! Backfill with the soil dug from the hole to the root flare level, then water in well. Add more soil if the backfilled soil settles. Don't press the soil with your foot or pound it down with your hands or shovel. It will just end up compacting the soil—especially clay soils—and possibly break roots. Water settles soil just fine. If a small depression is formed by the root-ball being a bit lower than the soil surface, you can use this for watering, like a saucer that slowly drains. As long as no roots are exposed, don't fill it in and risk burying the plant too deeply.

Don't fertilize a newly planted tree or shrub. They evolved to live off the litter of fallen leaves and twigs. It's a lean but

If your tree is balled-and-burlapped, place the root-ball in the prepared hole and then remove the burlap.

healthy diet. On the other hand, man-made hybrids like roses and rhododendrons that put on large and long-lasting floral displays do perform better if fertilized.

Planting in Containers

With the decrease in yard sizes and the increase in condominium, townhouse, and apartment living, more people are gardening in containers. In small gardens or on patios, a

Staking

Most annuals and perennials really don't need staking if you practice the "Chelsea chop" mentioned earlier. But large-growing dahlias do, as do many delphiniums, both top-heavy plants. It's best to stake dahlias when planting, keeping in mind to add one or two feet to the eventual height of the plant to calculate the height of the stake needed; the extra footage goes in the ground to provide anchorage. The same applies to delphiniums, though being perennial they will need to be staked each spring. One

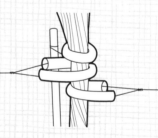

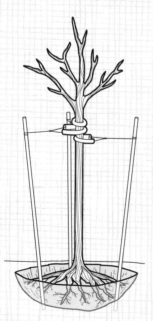

If necessary, stake a tree by placing three stakes angled outward around the trunk and loosely attaching the trunk by means of wires protected with sections of rubber tubing (scraps of old garden hose will do) where they encircle the trunk.

well-planted pot or container brings plants and flowers and their fragrances up close and adds a bit of excitement to the area. Container gardening also allows you the opportunity to experiment, to try new plants, to get to know a plant.

Experimenting with annuals in a container is an inexpensive and easy way to try out color and texture schemes on a small scale before expanding into the garden. If you want a year-round planting in your container, be sure to choose

sturdy stake per stem or four or five stakes around the clump, with cotton string or twine wrapped around the stakes and across the clumps at varying levels, will make an effective cage. This works very well for tomatoes, too.

Vines will need staking at first until they can reach and attach to the surface you provide. While it is their nature to twine, cling, or wind around something, they cannot do this if there is nothing there. Clematis or roses planted near the base of a tree will messily sprawl along the ground unless tied to a stake that leans onto the trunk, providing a guide to where the vine should go. Once there, the vine can go on its merry way with occasional guidance from you.

Shrubs don't need staking, but some trees may, especially if their top is disproportionately large in comparison to the root-ball. Stake a tree using three short stakes driven into the ground at an outward angle about three feet from the trunk, much like tent stakes. Run rope or wire through a piece of rubber tubing or old garden hose. Place the rubber tubing around the tree about two-thirds of the way up the trunk, in the branching area if possible. Tie the two ends of the string or wire firmly but not too tightly to one of the stakes. Do the same with the other two. Don't tie them so the tree is rigid and immovable. You want some looseness in the tension so the tree can sway some in the wind—this actually encourages root growth. If staked too firmly, a tree will never grow proper anchoring roots. I rarely stake a tree, as I buy small ones up to six feet tall and lightly branched. These establish better and more quickly—and being so small and open they won't be uprooted or tilted by the winds.

frost- or freeze-resistant containers and plants. Evergreen plants are best, especially ones with variegated leaves or colored stems to provide interest in winter when many plants are not in flower. Just be aware that trees and larger shrubs rarely grow to their normal heights in containers because of the restricted root area and that plants in pots are less cold hardy than they would be in the ground.

Drainage holes in the bottom of the pot are essential. No need to cover the holes with bits of broken pots or anything else, except perhaps a small piece of window screening to keep soil from washing out and slugs and worms from crawling in and hiding out. Nor is it necessary to fill the bottom two or three inches deep with gravel to help with drainage, another old saw trotted out from the days when soil dug right from the ground was put in pots. Today's potting soils drain perfectly well without anything extra in the bottom.

If a container does not have a drainage hole and you cannot or will not drill one in it, it is a cachepot (pronounced KASH-pet or KASH-poe)—a decorative container to hold a flowerpot with a drainage hole in it. If you use a cachepot, check often that it has not filled with water, drowning the plant in the container. You will have to take the flowerpot out and tip over the cachepot to drain out excess water at times. A few pieces of charcoal in the bottom help keep the excess water from souring and stinking, but not forever.

In the garden, a container can be set directly on the ground. But if the container is on a patio or balcony or deck, staining the surface beneath or dripping down on your guests or neighbors may be a concern. Besides a cachepot, many kinds of saucers can be used to catch excess water. You can choose from saucers made of glazed or unglazed terracotta, heavy duty plastic, metal, or thin clear plastic. All have their pros and cons, but the most important factor is how they look to you. Once a saucer is full, be sure to empty it. If the container is too big to lift, a turkey baster works wonders in removing the unwanted water.

Sometimes a container set on a flat surface doesn't drain well because the two surfaces seal against each other. If this is the case, you can lift the pot off the surface by using pot feet made of pottery, stone, metal, or rubber in decorative shapes like lion or dragon heads, flowers, or in the shape of Victorian high-heeled shoes. The rubber ones can slip under the pot out of sight and make the container appear to float just above the surface. Blocks of wood work just as well, but the best way to prevent staining is to use a saucer held up on unglazed terracotta feet, which rarely leave stains and which breathe, thus diminishing any rot potential.

If you want to lessen the weight of a large container, stack old plastic pots upside down and on top of each other, if needed, in the bottom of the container. Toss a little slug bait in the bottom before adding the soil (especially if you don't cover the drainage hole with screening to discourage slugs from climbing in) and fill with soil to the height required to cover the largest plant's root-ball. Don't use styrofoam "peanuts" in the bottom to save weight. They are a mess to clean out when repotting, and many now are biodegradable, turning into a soggy, drain-blocking mess the first time you water.

Just remember that no plant can stay in one pot indefinitely and live. Unless it is repotted into a larger pot or has some if its roots removed and the soil replenished, it will choke itself to death. This may take anywhere from one to ten years, but you will notice when it happens as the leaves and stems begin to die off in great numbers and it is difficult to even water the plant.

Thus, any tree or shrub of value planted in a container will, at some point, need to be repotted. Plants are easily removed from containers that have parallel, U-shaped, or V-shaped sides, but if the container has a lip that folds inward, you will not be able to get the plant out of the container without severely damaging or destroying its root-ball or destroying the container. If the lip folds in no more than the circumference of the bottom of the pot, it may be possible to saw out the plant and remove it like a plug. This does not work well if the top and bottom are very small, as there will be little of the plant left to unplug. You also need a saw long enough to reach the bottom of the pot. Keep these things in mind when placing a tree or shrub you want to keep for several years in a container. Also make sure the pot will be large enough to counterbalance the actual and potential top growth of the tree; otherwise, it will blow over with every windstorm.

Most outdoor containers are made of fired clay (glazed or unglazed—I include ceramics in this category), wood, plastic, fiberglass, metal, or concrete/cement. Each type has its good and bad points.

Terracotta pots

PROS: Terracotta pots are traditional looking; the color is warm and natural; the root zone breathes; standard sizes are available in quantity.

CONS: Low-fired cheap kinds break apart in freezing winters; they are heavy; if not soaked in water before potting they will wick water away from the soil; they become stained with salts, lime, and mosses on the outside.

Fired clay pots are the traditional container with their wonderfully warm rusty orange-brown coloring called terracotta. Unless they have been high fired, they will flake and crack and gradually deteriorate in climates that experience freezing. If you aren't sure if a pot is high fired, give it a sharp rap with your knuckles. A high-fired pot should have a high, clear, bell-like ring to it. A dull or hollow sound means the pot is low fired or has a crack in it. Do not assume that a highly decorated terracotta pot is high fired.

Expect to pay more for a high-fired pot, sometimes three to four times the price of a low-fired one. In time the investment will pay off because the high-fired pot should last many decades while the lower-fired ones will last but a few years, especially in cold climates. But note that even high-fired pots cannot be left out all winter in areas that experience prolonged, hard freezes, or alternating hard freezes and thaws, so you may want to bring them in during the winter or cover them with a decorative waterproof covering.

Should you seal a low-fired terracotta pot? There are products made specifically for sealing terracotta pots to keep them from absorbing water as it is the expansion and contraction of water during freezing that causes flaking and cracking. Read the label to see if a sealant is applicable to terracotta and make sure the pot is very dry before using the sealant.

Any unsealed terracotta pot should be soaked in water or somehow hydrated before you plant in it. Otherwise it will act like a wick and suck much of the water away from what you plant. It's easy with small containers but problematic with large ones. To hydrate a large container, leave it out in the rain for several days, or fill it with potting soil and keep the soil very wet for a couple of days, letting the container draw water from the soil. When the outside looks damp, you can plant.

Glazed pots

PROS: Glazed pots are colorful as a container or as a decorative object on their own, are better able to withstand freezing, and come in a variety of affordable prices.

CONS: They are heavy; colors are difficult to match if buying at different times; they may be damaged by freezing weather; higher-quality containers can be expensive and targets of theft.

As with terracotta pots, there are low-fired and high-fired glazed pots, though generally a glazed pot has to be fired at a higher temperature than terracotta to produced the glaze. But if the clay used to make the pot is porous or of poor quality, it too may crack in freezing weather. Sealing the inside of a very dry pot will help. The knuckle rap test works on glazed pots, too.

Glazed pots come in so many colors and shapes that they can be used by themselves in the garden or on a patio as a decorative element. If you want a pair or sets of pots that match, buy them at the same time so they come from the same glaze batch. Just like yarn colors, pot colors can vary with each batch of glaze.

High-quality glazed pots should be able to withstand freezing, but I wouldn't take the chance since they are expensive. Bring them in for the winter. In areas of mild winter weather with minimal freezing, if you must leave them out, empty them of soil to help protect against freeze damage. And if they are in a location that gets any public traffic, be sure they are well attached to a structure or the ground to deter theft—a concern with any expensive-looking pot. Or buy very inexpensive ones that will be cheap to replace.

Wooden containers

PROS: Wood planters are cheap, lightweight, can be made in any shape or size needed, and can be painted or re-painted to match any color scheme; they can be made of rot-resistant woods; wine barrel containers are usually of a consistent size whenever you need them.

CONS: "Redwood" types are small and poorly made and will have only a year or two of use; "wine barrels" may be cheap imitations; wood, unless properly treated or rot re-sistant, will deteriorate rapidly; antique lead-lined wood-en containers can be expensive.

Wooden containers include hanging baskets or long, nar-row containers made of or to look like redwood; wine bar-rels cut in half and charred on the interior (fake ones aren't charred); and other wooden containers made of various woods in squares, rectangles, or narrow troughlike shapes, painted or unpainted, sealed or unsealed.

The common small "redwood" containers found in nearly every garden center are, for the most part, cheaply made and will fall apart within a year or two as the fiberglass band and cheap metal clasps give way. Many hanging baskets come with a thin particle-board bottom. These are one-use wonders and probably not even good for green waste disposal because the "redwood" is a cheaper wood with a redwood-color stain on it.

The long, narrow trough types may last a year or two longer but are so narrow and shallow as to be useless except for planting the smallest of annuals. Many people put them on their balcony railings, which is usually against condominium and apartment rules and makes them potential skull crackers when wind, a guest, or the cat bumps them off the railing. If you are going to use a container on a railing, make sure the railing is sturdy enough to hold a container filled with soggy soil, that you can securely attach the container to the railing, that it's legal to have there, and that you have good homeowner's insurance.

Other wooden containers can be very sturdy and are sometimes treated with a preservative or sealer. If they are treated, inquire if they are safe for growing plants you intend to eat. Most come in larger sizes and with proper care will last for several years if made of cedar or other rot-resistant woods. They can be left to weather naturally or painted, though some that come oiled may not take any paint or stain. Ask when you purchase what was used to treat the wood, then go to the hardware store armed with that information and ask what is for sale to paint over that.

The price for ready-made containers is comparable to that of middle-range terracotta and glazed pots. Custom-made wooden containers cost more but offer more choices in the type of wood, shape, and finish. They can be made to fit in your garden or on your deck or patio or by the front door and painted to match the house color scheme. When made of high-quality rot-resistant woods, sealed, and painted, they will last for decades. A quick check of the antique planter market on the Internet will prove that.

Wooden wine or whiskey barrels cut in half across the middle make excellent containers for informal or rustic gardens—or if you own a vineyard. They will last for many years if not allowed to dry out. They are often a good bargain when on sale, especially at the big-box stores, but make sure they are real wine barrels and not just wooden containers made to look like them. The latter will not last as long as a real wine barrel. A real wine barrel will be charred on the inside, not just painted black or scorched. If you live near a winery or whiskey distillery, ask if there are any old barrels for sale, then cut them in half yourself.

While lighter than most clay pots when empty, wooden containers can be just as heavy when filled with soils.

Plastic containers

PROS: Plastic containers are uniform in size, lightweight, cheap or free from neighbors or nurseries, and long lasting if of high quality; they won't rot or break in frost.

CONS: They are plastic and look like plastic unless very high quality; in many areas they can't be recycled if any color other than black.

Plastic containers are the ones most commonly used in the horticultural industry to grow plants for sale. They are inexpensive and lightweight, come in uniform sizes, and can be reused. But they only come in basic black or more recently in hideous "trade" colors with brand names emblazoned across them, making them hard to use or even to recycle. That said, the typical black pots are excellent for use when raising your own plants. Larger five- to fifteen-gallon containers are ideal for growing tomatoes. The black plastic absorbs heat, giving the tomatoes, peppers, eggplants, and other heat lovers the extra warmth at the root level that they need to grow well. Conversely, any plant needing cool roots—such as Japanese maples, Himalayan blue poppies, and clematis, to name a few—will fry at the roots if they are left in full sun in such a pot. Provide some sort of shade around the pot, even if just by surrounding it with other pots.

Sun can damage these commercial containers over time, making them brittle so they shatter easily, but replacement and repotting is relatively easy. Just gently slip the plant from the old pot and place it in a new pot of the same shape and size. In most instances the roots will never be disturbed.

Many nurseries and people throw away the smaller pots or nonblack pots, so it's easy to get a free collection of them. The larger sturdy black plastic commercial pots are expensive and often reused by growers, so don't expect to get used ones free from a nursery; but if you have neighbors who just bought a bunch of trees in large sturdy black plastic pots, be a good neighbor and offer to dispose of their empty pots.

Then there are plastic containers made for the decorative market. These come in a variety of shapes, colors, and sizes. Some look like plastic, while a few cleverly colored and textured ones fool the eye. The price for a good-quality plastic container will be about the same as for a high-quality pottery or wooden one, but the plastic container will last for a long time and will not be subject to damage by frost or rot. Colors may fade in the sun. Inquire about the stability of the color.

Fiberglass containers

PROS: Fiberglass containers are strong, durable, and more colorfast than plastic; they come in a variety of shapes and colors; they can be made to look like other materials.

CONS: The price may be higher than for comparable plastic containers; harsh power washing or animals or people scratching on them can cause fraying of the fibers.

Fiberglass containers are similar to plastic ones but may hold colors better. The best kinds can be made to look convincingly like terracotta, concrete, stone, or metal. They may cost more; the fluctuating price of oil affects the production costs of all containers in different ways. And they are stronger than plastics.

Metal containers

PROS: Metal containers can be lightweight; they come in uniform shapes and sizes and colors; galvanized garbage cans are inexpensive and may annoy neighbors who need annoying.

CONS: Cheaper metals rust out and are easily dented; they are toxic and expensive if made of copper or lead; they can be heavy if made of thick and heavy metals; they can become very hot if in full sun; shiny trash can kinds can cause neighbors to make disparaging remarks, which may upset owners with thin skins or no sturdy belief in their own style choices.

Lead has been used for centuries for containers. It has a nice patina and lasts for centuries, and it doesn't conduct heat to the roots. Of course, today we know it can leach toxins into the soil. Most lead containers today are sold in the antique market at very high cost. Rare is the general gardener who has or can afford a lead container. Most metal containers are of galvanized tin or steel, or sometimes copper—but with the price of copper, I rather doubt most gardeners can afford one, much less want to have a copper pot on display to entice thieves.

A good container for modern-style homes and gardens is a galvanized trash can. To each his own, but I like them, though the idea wasn't mine. Drill holes in the bottom for drainage and plant away. They come in various sizes and usually a uniform shape. Galvanized metal farm watering troughs, available at farm supply stores, can be used in the same way.

Sheet metal containers are a modern fad. Lightweight, easy to shape into geometric forms and to paint with different colors, they are reasonably priced in comparison to other pots. How long will they last? It depends on the metal. Cheap metals soon rust out, dent, or bend. But if you prorate the cost over a couple of years, a metal container is a good value compared to the cost of the hundreds of frothy lattes the average person drinks in one year. They do heat up the soil, potentially causing trouble for heat-sensitive plants.

Concrete containers

PROS: Well-made concrete containers will last for decades; color mixed into the concrete will last for decades; they come in classic designs and styles.

CONS: They are very heavy; cheaply made ones won't last but a couple of years; color stains applied to the outside will need periodic maintenance; they are expensive; they leach lime, which stains colored concrete.

Concrete containers have been around for centuries. The Romans made them and many still can be found in museums. When properly made, they are resistant to most abuses except a direct blow from a sledgehammer, a speeding locomotive, or a badly driven auto. Poorly made brands will crumble in harsh winters as quickly as cheap clay. In this case you do get what you pay for.

They can be stained. However, unless the stain is mixed into the concrete with the cement it will fade over time and have to be reapplied to the surface. Covering the stain with a paste wax will help preserve the color for a few years longer.

Concrete containers are very heavy, needing to be placed on solid foundations. Rooftops and balconies are not the best place for them. Shipping will be a large part of the cost unless you are patient and can wait for your container to arrive by truck or ship.

Pruning

Newly planted trees and shrubs need little, if any, pruning. Limit pruning to cutting off broken, damaged, or dead branches and twigs for the first few years unless you are making a hedge. Every limb and branch that produces leaves produces that many more roots, helping to establish the plant. Once the plant is established, you can begin to prune for shape or to raise the crown of a tree to make the trunk taller, for instance. The height where a branch emerges on a trunk is where it will be the rest of its life. Branches don't move upward as the tree grows—a popular misconception. It's only the tip of a tree that moves upward by placing cell upon cell, in the sense of one brick on top of another.

Over time, the end of a branch will sag below the height of the branch's origin at the trunk due to the sheer mass of limbs it has to support. If a branch sags lower than you want, remove a few outer twigs and limbs and the branch will rebound. In some instances you will have to remove the whole branch at the trunk. See a good pruning book for advice on how to do that. It is important to prune away a branch at its origin. Don't leave a stump and don't bother painting the wound with anything. It will heal faster if nature has its way. Nor should you worry about "bleeding," which is simply sap running out. It will stop, or it will even seal up the cut in a few cases. If this so-called bleeding were truly detrimental, there would be few trees left in the woods after a windstorm.

Supplies to Keep Your Garden Growing

To maintain your financial and emotional investment in plants, you need to know the value and proper use of water, mulches, and fertilizers in the garden. You also need to know something about pesticides and their use. A final supply you might want to invest in is plant labels to jog your memory when years have passed since you first planted your perennials, shrubs, and trees.

Water and Watering Equipment

Once you put your plants in the ground, they will need to be watered, at least while getting established. For most trees and shrubs—and some perennials—that means never letting the plant dry out for the first three years it is in the ground. In milder climates, that means during the winter, too. The day you plant is the day you start counting the three sets of 365 days. Whenever I say "years," people invariably hear "summers," which is why I now say "three sets of 365 days." That gets a person's attention if only because it sounds bizarre. Do not think that autumn planting lets you off the hook regarding watering, especially in mild winter areas. It doesn't. You may not have to water but you have to be checking to be sure the root-ball is not drying out.

Newly planted evergreens that have tops wider than the root-ball actually create a rain shadow requiring you to water beneath the plant—not around it—to keep the root-ball moist until the roots have had about three years to grow out beyond the drip line created by the outside edge of the branch tips. It's also important to understand that plants near a wall or fence, or under an eave, might also be in a rain shadow. To test if your plant is getting enough water, simply dig a small hole near it about a foot deep. If the soil is moist at the bottom, all is well. If only the top inch or so is moist, you need to water slowly and deeply to get water down to at least a foot deep, allowing the plant's roots to establish themselves in cool, moist soil and better withstand droughts. (See "The Art of Watering.")

As water becomes a more precious resource, you want each drop to count. This is why you need to consider carefully when selecting watering equipment. Do you use a watering can or a soaker hose? How about a moveable sprinkler? Do you really need to have an irrigation system installed?

Watering buckets and cans

A large plastic bucket is very useful when you are moving large amounts of water to a newly dug hole. It's also good for mixing up fertilizers or chemicals. Just make sure you use one bucket for each. It helps to mark each bucket with indelible ink or paint each one with the words *water*, *fertilizer, herbicide, pesticide,* or *fungicide.* For most watering, use a watering can. This is any container with a handle, a hole at the top for filling, and a spout with or without a rose at the end, the rose being the round end with lots of little holes in it where the water comes out.

For watering plants, purchase a sturdy watering can—plastic or metal—with a removable rose that screws on or off. If you get one with a rose that pulls off or pushes on, make sure it holds very well. You don't want it popping off and causing a tidal wave of water to wash a bunch of seedlings from their flat. Various types of rose heads allow for coarse sprays for established plants, or fine sprays for newly sown seed or young seedlings. Some rose heads face out, some up, and some in odd directions. Avoid the latter. Those that face upward deliver a gentler spray for watering flats of seedlings and even large plants. I prefer them.

There are as many types of watering cans as there are designers. Stick to the basics. Choose a can that is well balanced when full of water, has a smooth handle (especially on the underside, so that it doesn't rub raw or cut your hand), and has a long spout so you can reach deep into the garden or pot. The spout should rise to be level with the top opening used for filling. If the end of the spout is below that, the water is likely to come spilling out every time you lift the can. I recommend buying plastic or galvanized metal. Unless a metal can is stainless steel or galvanized, it's likely to rust out at the seams. Rinse out a watering can after using liquid fertilizers, which all contain salts of some sort, to prolong its life.

Most watering cans hold one to three gallons of water. I use a small one that holds just one gallon to water small pots, indoor plants, and small seed flats. It fits under the faucet in the kitchen sink so is easy and quick to fill. For established or larger plants in the garden, I use a bigger watering can.

Large buckets, barrels, or trash cans filled with water and hidden in faraway parts of the garden can serve as reservoirs you can dip your watering can into for a quick refill without having to drag the hose out all the time or run back and forth to the house for more water. Keep such reservoirs securely covered to keep mosquitoes from breeding and for the safety of pets and children.

Hoses

Not all watering can be done with a can or a bucket. This is where hoses are ever so handy. (In the United Kingdom, hoses are called hose pipes.) A good, simple, flexible hose

The Art of Watering

Here are the key points of the art of watering:

» Know your soil and whether it holds water or drains quickly.

» Choose plants for your climate, soil, and water budget.

» Water slowly and deeply to establish plants.

» If water is running out of the container or garden onto sidewalks and driveways, you're watering too fast or too much.

» Once you've established a plant (usually after it's been in the ground for three years), it should not need artificial irrigation again except during a severe drought and only then if it might die from lack of water. If you don't believe this, read the wonderful books *Beth Chatto's Woodland Garden* and *Beth Chatto's Gravel Garden*.

If you are growing plants in mixed beds or are growing trees and shrubs, a series of soaker hoses laid out in the bed or over the root-balls of the trees and shrubs is all you need. The soaker hoses can be run manually or with a timer. While getting established, plants need several hours of a slow drip—from every couple of days to every two weeks, depending on how fast your soil drains and the air and soil temperature during the active growing

is indispensable in the garden. As with all equipment, buy good quality. A hose should remain flexible and kink free, be heavy duty, have well-made brass fittings at each end, and come with a lifetime or very long-term guarantee. (Save your receipt and the paper packaging!)

Hoses come in many lengths, from fifteen to one hundred feet or more. The length you need is your decision, but you should have enough length in one or more hoses to reach the farthest end of your garden without straining the hose at either end. I prefer one long hose and a couple of shorter ones. These can be hooked together for one super long hose or I can use a short, lightweight one for watering not too far from the spigot.

Hoses are made of plastic, vinyl, and high-quality rubber

season. This will encourage the roots to go deep toward the cool, moist zones of soil.

To give you an idea of how long it takes to water a bed or a tree properly and deeply enough, turn on a hose so it delivers a tiny trickle of water at a drip . . . drip . . . drip speed, like a very small leak. Place the end of the hose in a gallon can and time how long it takes to fill up the can. That's the minimum amount of time it takes to water a plant deeply enough into the soil for the roots to find the coolth and moisture they need to survive.

Hand watering is best done slowly at the base of the plant needing water. Standing in the garden waving a spray nozzle around makes you a garden ornament, not a good waterer.

When you are watering a pot, if the water runs out of the drainage holes right away it is very possible that the root-ball has dried out and is not absorbing the water. Rehydrate the soil by letting water trickle at the base of the plant stem; or if the plant is in a small pot, sink the pot into a bucket of water all the way to the rim of the pot and hold it down until air bubbles stop bubbling up. Pull out and let drain. Now the soil is rehydrated.

When you buy a watering can, pay attention to the rose (which should be removable): rose heads that face upward, like the one on the left, deliver a gentler spray than heads that face out.

like the kind used on roofs (often referred to as EPDM rubber). Plastic ones are a waste of time and money. They crack and break too soon for the investment. Reinforced vinyl with a high number of plies (layers like a car tire has) are very good, often come with a lifetime or long-term warranty, and are not too costly. Check for brass fittings; the better and stronger made they are, the less chance of blowouts. The best hoses are made of high-quality rubber and will last two, three, five, or ten times longer than vinyl. They won't degrade in the sun and they don't kink, but they are heavy to drag around. They are best for bringing water to the farthest reaches of the garden, much like having a temporary pipe laid out; you can add a high-quality, lighter-weight vinyl hose at the end for dragging around. Most of my watering is limited and general, so I prefer the reinforced high-quality vinyl hoses advertised as "kink free" or "kinkless."

To store a hose during seasons when it's in use, a large, sturdy winding spool next to the faucet is a good choice. Just make sure it is big enough for all the hose you are using and strong enough to handle the weight and pull of the hose as you wind it onto the spool. It should attach securely to the wall with long screws. Some people use old car wheel rims, draping the hose over them in large loops. Others just drape the hose over a large, sturdy L-shaped bracket. Fancy or clever isn't necessary.

When storing hoses for winter, stretch them out on a little slope to drain them thoroughly. Roll them up from the top of the slope, pushing the last bit of water down to drain out the far end. Draining is especially important in climates that freeze or when you store the hose in a building and don't want puddling to damage floors or walls.

Nozzles and wands

Hand nozzles with a squeeze trigger are what most people use at the end of a hose, but after years of watering with a wand in nurseries, I prefer wands and wouldn't use a hand nozzle again, even with all their dials for coarse, fine, stream, or broad stream. They just do not work as efficiently or give as much control of the flow of water, in my opinion. Wands are long metal (usually aluminum) tubes that attach to the end of a hose, used with a shutoff valve between the hose and the wand or on the wand itself. At the other end is a rose, either fixed or removable. Plastic roses are cheap but they chip easily, so I recommend spending the money for a good brass one. If a wand you are considering does not come with an on/off valve, purchase a good brass valve that screws into the wand at one end and the hose at the other.

Nozzles at the end of a hose are best used for filling watering containers, spraying down an area, washing a car, or power washing driveways, sidewalks, and patios. Tightened just so to allow a slow dripping of water, a nozzle can substitute for a soaker hose. If you prefer to use a nozzle, you can choose between two basic styles—those with a squeeze control grip and those that let you adjust the spray by twisting the nozzle. Get a sturdy one with various settings or that screws open or closed to allow variation in water flow. If you want to power wash your driveway or patio, buy a good brass high-pressure nozzle. Just remember that it can create enough pressure to peel paint off a wall or shred a plant. Use carefully.

Many manufacturers now make nozzles, wands, and hoses that connect to each other with a snap-on coupling. These are ideal for people whose hand strength is limited or who prefer the simplicity. As always, buy sturdy, well-made, easy-to-use, guaranteed products. Stay away from flimsy plastics. Most rely on a system where you pull back on a ring on the hose, insert the item you are attaching, and then let go of the ring, which snaps firmly back in place, locking the two pieces together. These couplings are also ideal to put on faucets in tight places where screwing on a hose would be impossible or hand wrenching.

Soaker hoses, drip systems, and soaker bags

For watering lawns, flower beds, and newly planted shrubs and trees, a nozzle or wand is of little use. Few of us can stand still long enough to deliver enough water at a slow enough rate to do any real good. This is why soaker hoses are so important—because they are the best way to slowly and deeply water newly planted trees and shrubs until established. Often made of old tires, these rough black rubber hoses seep water gently and slowly into the ground through numerous small pores. As water becomes more precious, this way of watering makes even better sense, ensuring that each drop you use in the garden is actually going to the plant deep in the ground and not evaporating or running off.

Soaker hoses come in many lengths and can be connected to a regular hose to stretch across a lawn to a bed. Make sure your water system has enough pressure to deliver water all the way to the end of the soaker hose at a steady pressure. Most city water mains do. Private wells may not. The easiest way to find out is to attach the hose to a spigot and see if water leakage is evenly distributed.

Soaker hoses are very flexible, making them easy to wind through a bed or in a spiral around the base of a tree. I suggest covering the hose with mulch to further preserve the water and to slow down the sun's rays from degrading the rubber. Maintaining a couple of inches of mulch over the hose is sufficient.

Like soaker hoses, drip or emitter systems deliver water slowly, but in this case directly to the plants needing the water and nowhere else. You can lay the system out yourself and cover with mulch, or have a professional install it. I do worry that such a focused system on a tree or shrub does little to encourage the roots to move out of the watered zone, so make sure a few emitters are outside of the rootball area to entice the searching roots to quest farther out.

The seeping sacks or soaker bags that hold three to twenty gallons of water are placed at the base of a newly planted tree and slowly release the water for half a day or more. They are very good investments—as long as you keep them filled with water.

Sprinklers

Whether oscillating, rotary, or pulsating, portable sprinklers are best used for lawns and vegetable gardens. Oscillating sprinklers are good for spreading water somewhat slowly and evenly over a wide rectangular area. Rotary sprinklers deliver water in a circular pattern, but I think they deliver too much water too fast and often leave corners unwatered. A pulsating sprinkler, often on a tall pipe on a tripod base for support, does a good job of delivering water, especially over an object like a fence or shrub to plants on the other side. It can be adjusted to water in a circle or in pie wedges of various sizes, making it useful for focused watering. I have often used an oscillating or a pulsating sprinkler over large planting areas when a soaker hose wasn't available or water pressure was insufficient, but I let them run for several hours as long as the water was staying within the planted area.

Whichever kind of sprinkler you use, a goodly portion of the water is lost to evaporation. Also, if the water starts running off the soil that means it is coming out too fast and not going into the soil and to the plants' roots. Regulate the tap so all the water spraying out is absorbed into the soil and not running off down the sidewalk or driveway, neither of which will grow with extra watering.

Irrigation systems

Irrigation is a tricky subject. My experience is that if you are growing plants in mixed beds and don't have a lawn or need a perfect lawn, you don't need to install an irrigation system. The best use of an irrigation system is for lawns, not for trees and shrubs unless emitter heads can be placed near the base of a tree or shrub and run for long periods of time without the other zones running too (which could flood the garden).

After years of hearing tales of woe from customers and friends about weak, dying, or dead plants where sprinkler systems have been used, I have concluded that sprinkler systems are the greatest threat to trees and shrubs, even more of a threat than improper planting. Frequent shallow watering forces the roots of plants up toward the surface where they will dry out faster in hot weather. Besides, constant irrigation at five, ten, or fifteen minutes a day is a waste of water, gets expensive, and means you've put water-hungry plants in an area that is too dry.

If you decide to go with an irrigation system, have a professional install it. Insist on the system having flexible placement, changeable nozzles or emitters, independently controlled zones for each planting area, and a good guarantee. An irrigation system should be drained before winter so it won't freeze and burst.

If you have already installed or inherited an irrigation system, let it run for a couple of hours or more to get in a good deep soaking. As long as no water is running down the drive or onto the sidewalk, you are watering well. If there is run-off, you need to rethink your system and modify it. Long, deep soaks spaced out over long periods of time are ideal. These deep soaks once or twice a week in normal rainless periods will do more good for new plants than little daily sprinkles. In an established garden, save the deep soakings for once or twice a month if needed.

Mulch

Mulch works hand in hand with water to keep your plants moist. Mulching simply means covering the ground with a layer of something to keep down weeds, hold in water, and prevent erosion. Unless you are planting on a steep slope, the best mulches are compost (made of decayed leaves, stems, and such) or products like compost but containing manures or rotted wood. It is important to note that there are feeding mulches and nonfeeding mulches—they are not the same.

Many people have not the room, inclination, strength, nor materials to make a compost pile. Fortunately, selling compost and mulch of all kinds is a big business and you can go to your local nursery, garden, or hardware store, even grocery stores in season, and purchase compost and other kinds of mulch by the bag or by the truck load at some places. The latter can be dumped in the drive for you to shovel and haul into the garden, or some companies will blow the compost

How to Read the Ingredients Label on Bags of Mulch

You read the ingredients label on any bag of potting soil, compost, or planting mix as you would a food label. Ingredients are listed in the order of their predominance, so that the first ingredient makes up the largest portion of the mix and each additional item constitutes less and less of the makeup of the mix. Potting soils and planting composts usually include composted wood products, which provide air spaces and encourage mycorrhizal growth, as the first ingredient; then compost, manures, or worm castings for natural nutrients; and pumice or sand to provide more permanent air spaces. Some still use peat moss for neutral moisture retention and bulk; some include organic or synthetic fertilizers for nutrition, and lime to "sweeten" the mix. Recently an extract of a particular yucca plant is being added as a natural moisture retention material instead of peat.

or mulch onto your beds, an excellent service when the garden is behind a big house with no alley, or with narrow walks or lots of stairs, or your back isn't up to the task.

Feeding mulches

Feeding mulches release nutrients into the soil as well as creating a beneficial environment for the microbiota in the soil. Microbiota are all the tiniest creatures—animal, insect, vegetable, and fungal—in the soil that decompose all matter, making nutrients available to plants or assisting plant roots in absorbing and using the nutrients. Feeding mulches include compost and rotted manures (including bat guano) alone or mixed with decomposed wood products such as bark, sawdust, or wood chips (see "How to Read the Ingredients Label on Bags of Mulch").

Compost is rotted plant material—leaves, flowers, stalks, twigs, branches, or chopped up bits. You can make your own (see "Making Compost") or buy it in bulk. The only addition to it might be lime to adjust the pH to neutral. Composted manures are the same as compost except that the plant material has first been run through the gut of some creature, then left to decompose further to reduce the high proportion of urea (urine), which can burn plant roots. Nothing else is added.

Mushroom compost, used to grow mushrooms, is compost that is a mix of any of these ingredients: straw, sawdust, manure, and sometimes lime. While used to grow mushrooms, the mixture composts further. When the mushroom growers are finished with it, it's especially good for roses, perennial borders, and vegetable gardens, particularly if it contains lime. It will not produce mushrooms for you, however.

Mixtures of all the above composts along with partially composted woody material and gypsum (believed to "open up" clay soils, but that theory is still open to debate) are sold as "soil builders" or cheaper mulches. They serve well as low-feed mulches and are ideal for mixing into or

Making Compost

Nature has been composting since—well, since nature was invented. It is the natural way plants are fed: their own leaves, stalks, stems, and branches fall to the ground around the plants and rot, releasing nutrients back into the soil a little bit at a time. Making compost is not difficult, though it takes some thought and physical activity to do it right. Microbes, fungi, insects, and worms do most of the work.

The easiest way to make compost is to create a bin of some sort with air holes in the side. It can be as simple as four posts about six feet tall pounded into the ground a foot or two, creating a square with three-foot-wide sides that is then wrapped with chicken or hog wire attached to all four posts. The end of the wire is hooked to the beginning post where the wire started, providing the door or gate to open so you can get the compost out when it's finished. A bin built from wood slats with quarter-inch gaps between each slat works well, too. There are also plastic bins made in all sorts of shapes and sizes.

And then there are barrels that are placed on a rotary spit-like stand with a flap door in the side through which you are meant to toss the material or remove the compost. You are supposed to turn the barrel a few times each day. I think this is too much work for too little payoff. But if you have a small space and need to turn out compost quickly, it has been known to work reasonably well for friends of mine who are very detail oriented.

Compost is made of any plant material: dead plants, living plants, wilted flowers, stalks and twigs, lawn clippings, leaves, vegetables scraps from the kitchen, crushed egg shells, even untreated cardboard and newspaper as long as any inks on them are black and soy based. Materials put in a compost bin are clas-

simply laying on top of clay soils and for plantings that include lots of woody plants mixed in with perennials, since they encourage the mycorrhizae needed for woody plants because of their high wood-based content.

Primarily wood-based mulches are less of a feeding

sified as either brown (dead plant materials, high in carbon) or green (fresh plant materials, high in nitrogen). Aim to add two to three times more brown than green by volume, though much depends on how wet or dry the materials are. The wetter the green, the less of it you use with the brown. Whether brown or green, don't use diseased materials, seed heads full of weedy seeds, or roots of very pernicious weeds, just in case the pile doesn't heat up enough to kill them off. Nor should you use clippings from a lawn that has been treated with a weed-and-feed product. The "weed" portion is a broadleaf herbicide that will remain active for a long time so that when you put the compost containing it on the garden it will continue to kill broadleaves—most perennials.

A "compost starter" product is not needed. If you have made your mixture properly, it will contain or quickly attract any microbes, bacteria, fungi, and other critters to enhance the project. Tossing in some old leftover organic fertilizer at less than half the rate recommended on its package will enhance the decomposition and encourage good microbes but isn't necessary. Too much organic fertilizer could kill the life in the compost, as could chemical fertilizers. A shovel of old compost or good soil will contain plenty of microscopic life to start the project if you think they are needed.

Oxygen is very important to oxidize the carbon, keeping the decomposition going. This is provided by turning the pile often, which loosens up the mix to create more air spaces. The final ingredient is water. Just as a dry paper bag or flower stalk doesn't decompose—though both may become brittle and crumble—neither will a dry pile of plant debris rot. Add just enough water

mulch but are important to helping trees and shrubs take in nutrients by encouraging symbiotic fungi to grow. These fungi break down the wood fibers and penetrate the tree or shrub roots, assisting in the exchange of nutrients and moisture back and forth. Very clever, these plants.

(Making Compost, continued)

to keep the pile moistened but not soggy, which could turn it anaerobic and stinky. Rain in season usually provides enough water, but a slow soak once in a while from the hose helps in dry weather.

Surprisingly (or shockingly to those of delicate sensibilities), urine from a healthy individual (not on antibiotics or other prescription drugs) is an excellent addition to the compost pile. It is high in nitrogen and other nutrients. For centuries many gardeners have discretely—or not so discretely—added the liquid contents of a chamber pot to their compost piles or encouraged their tea, coffee, or beer-drinking male friends at outdoor events to use the compost pile for quick relief. We'll pass on discussing the use of human manure. Some cultures use it and some don't. It's best not to use the manure of carnivores in compost (although see "zoo doo" in this chapter). On the other hand, good old-fashioned dairy, chicken, horse, rabbit, and llama manures and beddings, especially from organic farms, make wonderful additions to a compost pile as they all contain both green and brown elements.

It is very important to keep the temperature of the compost pile in the range of 135 to 160 degrees F to speed up the decomposition and to destroy weed seeds and pathogens. You create this temperature by building the pile with the proper ratio of brown to green, turning the pile often, and keeping it moist but not soggy. To make turning the pile easier, some people make three bins: the first for starting, the second to shovel the first pile into after a couple of weeks, and the third to shovel the contents of the middle pile into after a couple of weeks, where it rests and finishes decomposition into a black earthy-smelling crumbling material that gardeners call black gold.

Zoo doo and other animal manure mulches

Among the feeding mulches are "zoo doo" and other animal manures. Many zoos sell a product made of composted
manure from the zoo animals along with their bedding of hay,
straw, or wood products. Support your local zoo and buy it.
If you can get some from lions or tigers you'll surely keep the
neighbor's cats and dogs guessing—and out of your garden.

Llama manure is the only manure I know of that can be
used fresh, right from the llama. I have planted all sorts of
fall bulbs in fresh, wet llama manure mixed half and half
with soil with never a problem. Usually any contact with a
manure will rot a bulb in no time at all, but not the llama's.
In areas where there are llama farms you may be able to get
it by offering to haul it away.

Chicken and horse manures are very rich (high in urea)
so must be well composted and used sparingly. Horse
manures also have a high weed seed content. Good hot
composting should kill off most of the seeds. Both are good
for vegetable gardens—in small doses.

Pit-washed dairy manure is very popular in areas with
many dairies. It comes from the manured bedding material
that is removed daily from barns and "washed" to produce
liquid manures. The remaining solids are sold as pit-washed
dairy manure, usually by the dump-truck load. It still contains somewhat high levels of urea, but after it sits out in the
rain for a couple of days, urea levels are reduced enough to
allow use directly on planted beds. It's best used in perennial
and annual beds as a top application and in vegetable beds
well dug in. I have used it with great success in mixed borders infested with root weevils (a very annoying and destruc-
tive insect) and other unwanted insects. The remaining urea

seems to be sufficient to burn out weevils' grubs and their eggs, and slugs, too, but it rarely harms plants—except for burning new leaves of astilbes, for some odd reason.

I would not use pit-washed dairy manure on plantings primarily made up of woody plants—shrubs, conifers, or trees. Using dairy manure around or under azaleas, rhododendrons, or Japanese maples will burn the small, sensitive roots they have. I've also come to believe that placing manure near Japanese maples is the main reason for the rise in cases of verticillium wilt among them. This disease causes sudden wilting of the branches or outright killing of entire limbs or the whole tree. Some trees will live with this disease and show no signs of it, while others die straight away. It is known that manure and high fertility in the soils encourages the growth of this fungus in food crop fields. My suspicion is that it does the same in the garden, infecting susceptible maples by creating lush, succulent growth on the maples and also causing a huge increase of the fungus in the soil. I have been able to save several infected Japanese maples by removing manure mulches and making sure the plant is not stressed by drought or anything else and is not overfed with high-nitrogen fertilizers, which can seep into the root area of the tree from lawns above or around it.

Nonfeeding mulches

The most common form of wood-based mulch sold is bark, usually as either fine bark or nuggets. Both are useless as feeding mulches as they have not been decomposed. The former is only good as a weed-suppressing mulch. It's important to understand that these uncomposted bark mulches may also actually shed water or keep water from getting through to the soil, causing the soils they cover to dry out. I don't know what the wood nuggets really do, except look awful in the garden. Their appeal is appalling. They don't suppress weeds, they take years to decompose, and they wash or slide down hills in the rainy season.

The best nonfeeding mulches are chippings from a tree service grinder or chipper. If you see an arborist in the neighborhood cutting down and chipping up a tree, stop by and offer to let them dump the chips in your yard or drive. They don't have to haul it away, and you get a good mulch. Just be certain the tree being chipped is not diseased but was healthy or died of natural causes. That's my opinion. Some arborists and scientists say there's no worry. Well, I'm going to worry. Better safe than sorry. I don't want potential mad birch disease in my garden. Sawdust as a mulch is best used when well rotted. If not, it forms a hard crust and binds any nitrogen as it decomposes, keeping the nitrogen from plants.

Other natural nonfeeding mulches include pine needles, straw, cocoa shells, and husks. Pine needles are sold as mulch in areas with great pine forests. This mulch is good for woodland plantings around trees and shrubs and as a protective winter mulch, as it decomposes very slowly. It's not very good in any kind of perennial planting. Salt marsh hay is another mulch product, this one particular to coastal areas. It does not contain harmful levels of salt, despite its name. Don't use regular hay as a mulch—it has too many weed and grass seeds in it. Straw, the stalks left over from grain threshing, can be a good mulch. If any seeds are in it, they will be annual grains easily weeded out. Cocoa husks make your garden smell lovely but are best used for paths—as are nut husks or shells, which inevitably bring in squirrels and rats looking for the nuts. Use with caution.

Peat is often mentioned for use as a mulch, especially in older books and by writers who blithely quote from such works. It is, however, not a good mulch. Put dry on top of soil, it will remain hydrophobic, never holding any water, repelling it instead. It has no nutritional value—another negative. And there is the argument that peat harvesting is destroying a resource faster than it can regenerate and shouldn't be used at all. North American and Scandinavian peat harvesters say this is not a problem with their peat bogs, which they claim are made up of species that regenerate quickly when cut, like a lawn. Other European and Russian peat bogs are harvested more like mining operations, allowing no regeneration. The vast majority of peat in North America comes from Canada. It is up to you to make your moral choice in this instance. Personally, I see little need for peat in the garden so avoid the controversy altogether.

Gravels—crushed or washed—are excellent mulches for drought-tolerant gardens or plants needing free-draining and surface-warmer soils. Gravel mulches also keep moisture away from soil-level crowns of plants vulnerable to wet-season rotting. Like most mulches, gravels help retain any moisture that does get into the soil. Though plants may be drought-tolerant or dry loving, most still need access to small amounts of moisture and coolness even during the hot season. Some people and designers use large chunks of marble or stone or large rounded river rocks as decorative mulches. It is important to remember that these large stones don't keep weeds down so are difficult to keep clean and weed-free.

Man-made mulches like burlap, plastic, and landscape fabrics have very particular uses and I would advise against using them in any home garden plantings. However, one good exception is the use of untreated burlap for stabilizing slopes or hillsides until new plants can grow out and cover the slope. By that time the burlap will have rotted away.

Which mulches to use where

A study carried out several decades ago at the Arnold Arboretum in Boston found that mulches made of herbaceous materials—leaves, grasses, manures, and some little twigs and stems—are best used on perennial, vegetable, and annual gardens. Wood-based mulches with little or no manure in them are best used around woody plants or in woodlands. Like to like, as it were.

The study, and others like it, found that soil microbiota (all the microscopic critters and fungi in the soil that decompose the debris and assist the plants in taking up nutrients) are specific to either grasslands or woodlands. It makes sense. Grasslands are filled with flowers, grasses, and grazing animals, which return the grazed greens to the earth in rich manures. Those not ruminated just fall over and quickly decompose. Trees and shrubs, however, have evolved with very small herds of grazers or with just solitary animals that eat lots of wood-based foods, leaving smaller piles of nutrient-poor manures. Thus woodlands have evolved to rely on multitudes of mycorrhizae (fungi) to do the rotting and converting of dead, tough woody plant material into food; these fungi make food available to woody plants by actually penetrating the root tips of the trees or shrubs so that nutrients and water are exchanged between the two. Who would have guessed that such cooperation is hidden beneath our feet as we walk through forests?

Other studies suggest that when trees and shrubs are exposed to manures from grassland grazers, the manures increase populations of fungi and other bacteria that are harmful to the tree, now made vulnerable and soft by the rich feeding. Think about what would happen if we lived off only fatty foods, alcohol, and sugars: we would—we do—become more susceptible to diseases and illness.

Annuals and perennials and roses need to live a rich life to produce all those flowers for months on end. Woodland plants live a lean life. They should do the same in our gardens.

How to apply mulches

Apply feeding mulches two to four inches deep, depending on how dense the mulch is, with lighter mulches applied more thickly. Be careful not to bury the stems of woody plants or shallow-rooted plants like rhododendrons, azaleas, and Japanese maples. Never bury the stems of plants with gray hairy leaves, which have evolved in droughty areas (think of lavenders, salvias, and verbascums); mulches over them will cause rot to set in quickly. Never bury the eyes (resting buds) of a peony; you must always see its little pink or red eyes sitting right at ground level.

Don't worry about burying the graft union or even the stems of a rose, as so many books and rose organizations advise—or used to advise—against. Roses evolved to run underground in search of fresh nutrients. Bury a rose's stems a foot deep and it will just make roots along the stems and grow merrily on. However, when in doubt about what to bury or not to bury on any plant, err on the side of caution and keep the mulch away from the plant's crown.

Use chipped wood as a mulch six to eight inches deep around newly planted trees, but keep the mulch at least eight inches away from the trunk and mulch out to the drip line. Never bury the trunk with mulch, which will cause rot in most instances. Besides keeping down weeds and holding in moisture, mulch under a tree keeps lawn mowers and weed trimmers away from the trunk. Too many trees are killed by being hit by lawn mowers and weed trimmers. These hits bruise and eventually kill the bark, ringing the trunk with dead vascular tissue and shutting off all avenues for moving water and food back and forth from leaves to roots.

Fertilizers

Some perennials and annuals and all vegetables need fertilizers in addition to composts and mulches. You can usually tell if your plant is not getting enough nutrients: growth is spindly, leaves appear only at the tips, or leaves look chlorotic (yellow). These may be symptoms of other problems, too, but if you've supplied adequate water and light and the plant is still weak and a bilious color, think food. Perennials that produce lots of flowers and top growth or flower over long periods of time (think peonies, delphiniums, and geraniums) usually need more fertilizer than those from dry, rocky areas (lavenders, salvias, and anthemis, for instance).

Plants don't care whether their nutrients come from organic or synthetic sources. The term **organic** is misleading on a scientific level, but to the average gardener it means a product made from materials produced from or by animals, vegetables, or natural-occurring minerals. These fertilizers release their nutrients slowly, thus acting in a more natural way than synthetic fertilizers. Organics also feed the microbiota in the soil, while synthetics can introduce salts and decrease the needed microbiota if overused. I prefer to use organics as much as possible for the simple reason that they act more like nature.

I use and recommend synthetics if a plant needs a quick feed to stave off starvation or collapse, or to encourage a bit faster bulking up of a plant for division. But do use synthetics with care and caution, always following the directions on the package to avoid burning of roots. If the directions are not clear about where to place the fertilizer, whether in or on top of the soil, you usually will not go wrong if you spread the recommended amount over the top of the ground after planting and then water thoroughly to start washing the nutrients into the soil. Rains, further waterings, worms, and scratching birds will continue the process. I no longer put fertilizer in the bottom of a planting hole—too much work and I don't want to risk burning tender new roots even if the fertilizer says it won't burn. Nature nearly always renews the nutrients from the top of the soil, letting them leach downward.

A fertilizer label lists three main nutrients: nitrogen (N), phosphorus (P), and potassium (K). They are always listed in this order, using numbers that indicate the percentage by weight of each item in the mix. For example, 4:10:9 means 4 percent nitrogen, 10 percent phosphorus, and 9 percent potassium by weight are in the mix; the remainder is other macronutrients, micronutrients, and inert or nonfeeding materials (fillers). Macronutrients, along with NPK, are calcium, sulfur, and magnesium. Micronutrients are iron, copper, and manganese, to name a few, not unlike the vitamins many of us take. The label also lists fillers, which add bulk and something to bind the ingredients together, and various beneficial mycorrhizae and bacteria, not unlike what a yogurt label lists. These beneficials are no fad but an example of the organic movement and the fertilizer industry combining good sense and science.

The higher the nitrogen number, the more the fertilizer

will accelerate leaf growth. Lawn fertilizers are high in nitrogen. Phosphorus is for the all-round general health and growth of the plant, though it is often used to encourage root growth. Potassium helps a plant convert the various nutrients into forms the plant can use or helps it make food: chlorophyll, carbs, and proteins. High numbers, however, are not a good thing. Lower numbers are actually better because the mix is not so rich, nor is it as likely to pollute streams and lakes. Formulations will often vary to reflect the typical soil in an area. Alaskan soils hold and release nutrients differently from soils in Florida or Vermont and have different levels and types of nutrients.

You can overfeed with any fertilizers, making a plant a juicy meal for insects and an inviting site for diseases. Always follow the directions on the container and when in doubt use less. Soil mixes with fertilizers included are best for pots or beds of annuals—not for use on the ground among perennials, trees, and shrubs. Time-release fertilizers are best in very warm climates or in container plantings. In cool soils they feed too late into the season, releasing nutrients too slowly.

Trees and shrubs rarely, if ever, need fertilizer. In nature they live off low levels of nutrients in the native soil and the annual feedings from fallen, rotting leaves and twigs. This tells you that the only good horticultural reason to rake leaves and twigs away from beneath or around your woody plantings is if there are small plants that would be smothered by the mat of wet leaves under the snow or in spring. If the emerging plants look like they need help pushing through the leaf layer, you can do an early spring fluffing of the leaves with a steel leaf rake. Birds will soon be there, too, scratching about for insects and worms, breaking down the leaves even more and freeing any stuck shoots. Nature has done quite well without us for a few hundred thousand years. If you personally are offended by leaves on the ground around your shrubs or woodland plantings, just look the other way for a couple of weeks. Your garden will look fine when you turn back.

Pesticides and Herbicides

There was a time when chemicals were going to make our gardens—and our world—a better place. Times and attitudes have certainly changed, or at least marketing is much more subtle. Though chemicals still have a place in gardening, it is a much smaller and better-thought-out place. We have come to realize that instead of eliminating pests and diseases and weeds, we have, in many instances, created chemically resistant forms of all three and caused grave damage to the environment. Great debates rage on about the use of chemicals in gardens, but practically and accurately speaking, we use them all the time: fertilizers, even organic ones, are chemical in nature.

I take the middle road. There are times when a few bugs and diseases cause no harm except to our sense of pride and aesthetics. Leave them for the other creatures to eat or the plant to battle against. With proper feeding, siting, and moisture levels, your plants should not be bothered by most diseases and insects that set upon them. The best pesticide and herbicide is good old-fashioned prevention, mulching, and quick weeding before things get out of control.

Still, there are times when action is called for. Often a simple daily spray of water from the hose for a couple days will wash that bug right out of its lair. I also often just pinch off the infested soft tip growth the moment I notice it covered in sticky green aphids or bug spit. The plant simply sends out another shoot from the latent bud below the pinch. Many insects such as aphids and other sap-sucking kinds can be killed by applications of "soap" insecticides, usually, though not always, made of animal fats just like soaps were (or still are, in some cases). The greasy quality of the soap mixture smothers the insects, and then the soap washes off the plant. Other insecticides contain juices extracted from the pyrethrum daisy, nature's own nerve toxin; these attack an insect's nervous system to kill it. Natural and organic, but still toxic and to be used with caution.

For difficult infestations of persistent and damaging insects, we might have to resort to chemicals applied sparingly and with a focused aim, not sprayed about in all directions at the first sign of damage. It is important to know what it is you are fighting—whether an actual disease or pest, or just damage caused by weather, by someone or something running through a plant, or by another chemical like bleach running off from power washing your home. Don't assume any blemish or leaf discoloration is from an insect or disease and then start spraying everything wildly. Seek advice first!

It is the same with weed control. Start simply and cautiously. The first line of defense is not to let any weed get a hold in your garden. The old adage "one year seed, seven years weed" is oh so true. Nip them in the bud. Most seeding weeds are annuals, so if you pull off and destroy the flowers quickly the plant will die without reproducing. Using a thick mulch will keep most seeds from germinating. Any that do are easily plucked up by one hand while the other holds your beverage of choice. Then again, at the first sign of a pernicious perennial weed like creeping buttercup, crabgrass, or their ilk, you will need to put your beverage down, get on your knees, and pluck it out—every root and bit.

If any of these get away from you, spreading like vegetative wildfire, I'm all for using a well-aimed shot of a glyphosate-based herbicide. Again, aim well and use little. Those with an organic ethos can use the old kettle of boiling water trick where you pour the scalding water on the offending culprit, or get out the little propane torch you use to caramelize your crème brûlée and burn out the miscreant, but make sure you don't torch the yard or neighborhood. You see, whether "organic" or "chemical," there are dangers in all methods of weed and pest eradication when applied willy-nilly or with hysterics.

Whichever product you use, always read the label and follow the directions fully and carefully. I come from a long line of farmers and gardeners, and none of us want any more chemicals in our environment than you want. But when a chemical is needed, we know to use discretion, caution, and good sense. For further information on this vast and controversial subject, contact your local Master Gardener program or read up in a good organic gardening book like *Ann Lovejoy's Organic Garden Design School*.

Plant Labels

No matter how brilliant the gardener, how keen her or his brain, a time will come when the name of a plant will not come to mind or be found in a record book. This is where plant labels come in. Of course, just putting a label by a plant does not solve the issue when birds, frost, small rodents, teething puppies, creative or mischievous children, thoughtless help, or addle-brained garden visitors

steal, move, remove, chew, wrongly place, or misplace garden labels. Nor is a name written on something flimsy or in
ephemeral ink of help when the label crumbles or the writing fades. What to do? There are more than enough styles
of labels on the market, as well as markers. Whichever you
choose, make sure it is long-lasting and holds writing for
many years.

Wooden labels written on with sun-resistant ink or good
graphite pencils will last one season for annuals or vegetables in a bed. Use large flat stick-type labels, which take
longer to rot where they make soil contact. Clear nail polish applied over the writing helps prevent rapid fading or
washing off.

For more permanent labels, a good UV-resistant plastic
six-inch stick-type label works for several years if written
on in pencil—not ink of any kind unless you cover it with
a clear sealant. A good trick is to make two labels: one is
buried beneath the perennial plant (it doesn't work so well
with trees and shrubs, for obvious reasons) so that when
the time comes to dig up the plant for removal or division,
you'll find the name safely kept. The other label is placed on
a consistent side of the plant (north or south, back or front)
and pushed into the soil just to or below ground level. Doing
the latter makes less of a temptation for children, birds,
dogs, and nosy visitors. I have had such labels remain legible for nine years.

For labels that will last twenty to thirty years and still
be legible, use anodized aluminum labels written on with
a #2 pencil. I have discovered some in old gardens with
the completely legible name and planting date written on
them thirty-plus years earlier. They come in long stick-
type shapes, various T shapes, and with wires for tying

to branches. For the latter it is important to remember to check the wire every other year to make sure it is not cutting into the branch or already embedded in it, which can strangle the branch to death at worst or present a saw hazard at best.

Ignore those labels that let you "impress" the words upon a soft, thin metal plate wrapped around a piece of cardboard. The seal will leak within a year, the paper will rot, and the thin metal will warp or become scratched, rendering anything written on it illegible.

A #2 graphite pencil has been the most stable marker I have used in more than forty-five years. All inks fade. An etching tool is too elaborate for me. Paint flakes. Clear nail polish eventually erodes, exposing the ink below. Grease pens eventually fade and smudge. I cannot afford, much less find, those old machines that printed plant names in lead strips like those used by alpine plant gardeners in the 1920s and 1930s. So a #2 graphite pencil it remains.

What goes on the label?

» plant name—the minimum requirement
» date sown or acquired
» source of plant or seed

If you are a more intense gardener, you will also want to include these facts:

» reference number of the seed or plant if from a special collection or to refer to in your own reference records
» number of seeds sown or bulbs originally planted
» date of germination and how many seeds germinated

The best backup is a record book or simple drawing or list of plants in a garden area written on a piece of paper. You can make a very simple record by walking along a border or through the garden writing down the name of each plant as you go, noting whether on the right or the left and if near something permanent like a stone or pipe or post. This will narrow down the choices in future years when no one can remember the plant's name. Plus it provides a fascinating record of what you have grown over the years. I have simple blooming lists more than thirty years old written sequentially as I walked through a garden. These have proved invaluable for recovering the name of a plant or proving that a friend or I grew it that long ago.

Afterword

When I was first going to prune trees I read every book I could find, knowing full well once I made a cut I could not start over. No matter how many books I read, I did not gain any confidence. I turned to longtime gardening friend Aline Strutz to ask her what to do. Surely she who was a self-taught botanist and extraordinary gardener would have wise advice. She did, and it was simple and right: "Just do it, Jim!" In other words, I had the information, now I just needed the confidence of experience, and the only way to get that was to start pruning.

With this book I have given you the basic knowledge to allow you to "just do it!"—to set about making your own garden or improving the one you have. You just need the experience. Plants are always your best teachers, followed by neighbors with green thumbs and those true experts who speak and write from personal experience. Occam's razor applies in gardening, too: the simplest or most obvious advice is usually the right advice.

It is also okay to make mistakes, as long as you learn from them. I am many times saddened when a plant dies, especially if I had a hand in the cause of its death because of ignorance, or more likely stupidity. However, when a plant dies, you have the beginnings of a fine compost pile and will have learned an important lesson. Ask questions when you make a mistake **and** when you succeed, not only of yourself but also of your friends and other gardeners. Cooperative extension services in the United States are founts of knowledge, often managing the Master Garden programs. In any country, botanic gardens, public gardens, and garden societies offer a wealth of help, can point you in the direction of helpful organizations, and provide an opportunity for hands-on volunteer work.

When you have become a better gardener through experience, I hope you will share your successful techniques with your fellow gardeners, just as so many have done with me over the decades that I have been a gardener and horticulturalist. Because of the generosity of those individuals, I feel as if they are right there with me when I am in the garden, encouraging me to learn and just as thrilled with the successes or puzzled by the failures as I am. Gardening may be a solitary hobby at times, but it is never a lonely one.

Gardening is, some might argue but I truly believe, the greatest fraternity humankind has created. It is full of generous, fun, opinionated, eccentric, brilliant, and sometimes downright odd artists, craftswomen, and craftsmen. Through gardening they have brought together all of the arts, sciences, and crafts. They watch the leaves to know when it is warm enough to plant or time to close down the garden. They provide habitat for all sorts of creatures—good and bad. They create visual music and deeply meaningful—if at times arcane—symbolism with plants and form and sculptured or printed words. They understand the natural world, of which we are still so much a part. They have brought themselves back into the Garden of Eden or reached nirvana or become one with nature—and while so doing have remained firmly planted in the modern world.

Horticulture or gardening, whichever you wish to call it, is in my opinion the second greatest of the living arts, successful child rearing its only superior. Horticulture incorporates science, art, craft, nature, observation, emotion, and the fourth dimension of time. It has given, does give, and will continue to give great satisfaction to those who practice it. I hope that what I have written here may in some way, small or large, lead you to a point of success and of finding more pleasure in gardening. Plants, like the best of friends, a devoted pet, or a true loved one, don't judge you. I hope you can do the same as you garden: just accept the pleasures and education that it will bring you. Revel in the magic, and in the colors, the scents, the feeling of a job well done. Really do take the time just to sit and smell the roses and enjoy the sweet feeling of accomplishment and partnership with nature.

Acknowledgments

First I must thank the thousands of customers whom I have met, talked to, assisted, and been educated by over the past forty years—including those whom I have bemused or frightened, enthused or enlightened. It is they who have taught me what the general gardening public, novice or old hand, wants or needs, and how best to help them figure out what those things are. Customers continue to teach me. Thank you.

Second, I must tender thanks to the scores of nursery men and women and horticulturists around the world with whom I have worked or discussed what it is our industry does best and worst, where improvements are needed, and how to educate our customers. To all of them, my sincerest thanks for sharing their knowledge and experience. They remain nameless so I alone will take any flack for what I have written.

Tom Fischer, editor-in-chief at Timber, saw this book in me and set about to help me find and write it. Throughout the writing and editing process he graciously and firmly led the way, patient beyond belief. My sincere thanks to him for this, and for publishing my first national piece long ago in *Horticulture* magazine. In this vein, I also single out people who continually urged me to write, write, write over the years: Helen Hulbert, Pat Bender, Maryann Pember, Barbara Asmervig, Graham Thomas, and Roy Lancaster who in 2009 after a lovely meal and a couple of glasses of wine got all of this started by saying, "Just start writing, Jim!" Sound familiar?

My grandmother, Irene Benson, first taught me to plant when I was three, clearly seeing the gardening gene within me. She, along with my parents, Charlie and Arlene Fox, gave me garden space to indulge the whims and fancies of this passion for more than fifty years, ofttimes bemusedly. Remarkable and loving.

Early Alaska homesteaders created gardens of great beauty in the Far North long before people thought such things possible. I owe a great debt to them. Fanny Werner, a transplanted Englishwoman, in the 1930s created a lovely garden of mixed borders set off by a lawn and white picket fence backed by exotic and native trees. Aline Strutz, the best all-round horticulturalist Alaska ever produced, taught me to experiment, to learn from the plants, and to have the highest standards of cultivation and evaluation. She opened my eyes to what the world has to offer.

Virgil Eckert of Hillcrest Acres, Palmer, Alaska, taught me patience and the practical aspects of running a nursery where plants were grown in and dug from the field on order. Evelyn Bush, another self-taught horticulturalist with remarkable instincts, shared her secrets for growing annuals and vegetables of great quality, ready for sale the moment snow was gone from gardens, from her nursery, Bushes Bunches, also in Palmer, Alaska. Doug Tryck, of

Tryck Nursery in Anchorage, Alaska, an optimistic dreamer himself, made me look to the exotic and to keep dreaming of possibilities.

Betty Mears taught me a tremendous lot after her death, for I rented her empty home when I was nineteen, eight years after her passing, the garden long untended. Seeing so many exotic (to me) plants awaken in that garden the first spring, reading the many books and notes of hers I was given, and mining the memories of her friends, I learned what she had grown, her ideas, her hopes, and things others had forgotten or never even considered.

Alaska's best garden writer, Lenore Hedla, and her practical green-thumbed husband, George, encouraged me for many years—over many a glass of crisp chardonnay—to expand my horticultural horizons mentally, geographically, and literarily.

Another Alaskan, Nancy Cunningham, whose life has been a great optimistic adventure, taught me the sheer joy of gardening in the planting, the harvesting, and even the weeding. She also showed me it was great mental and physical therapy. Plants grew for her with chlorophytic joie de vivre.

It was Bernice and Allan Linn, also of Palmer, Alaska, who gave me a grand palette upon which to paint my first large garden fresco. It succeeded beyond my greatest imaginings and theirs.

Many other gardeners in Sweden, England, Wales, Scotland, Ireland, Canada, the Czech Republic, France, Germany, South Africa, and the United States—many experts in their fields—have been generous beyond belief in sharing their opinions and knowledge, proving again and again how wonderful gardeners as a group are. I have been able to meet and create long friendships with many, some my personal heroes. To them all—many, many thanks. Even as this is written more new friends are made, daily improving what I know.

My dear friend Diane Brenner generously gave of her time, and of her own interest in learning to garden, to read through the initial manuscript, offering much insightful advice. Jan Condit read the finished work, making fine points and giving much encouragement.

Writing is editing as much as it is writing. What a privilege it has been to work with Lorraine Anderson, copy editor extraordinaire. Very lucky is the author who has her as a collaborator and teacher.

Many other individuals have generously given time, plants, knowledge, and friendship to me over the years, making me a better horticulturalist, writer, and person. Heartfelt thanks to Ned, Lisa, and Wendy for endurance, patience, education and confidence. Special mention to Maryann and Charles, John, and Nita Jo for lending their tools for evaluation, though they knew not why. Many others know who they are and have my enduring thanks, also. Their belief in and support of me continues to humble.

While a host of guides have led me to this place in my life, everything I have written in this book I alone am responsible for. The opinions expressed herein do not represent any organization past or present for which I have worked nor any group of which I may be a member, unless specifically quoted.

Recommended Reading

(An extremely abridged list, I might add!)

Bender, Steve (ed.). 2004. *The Southern Living Garden Book*. Birmingham, AL: Oxmoor House.

Brenzel, Kathleen Norris (ed.). 2012. *The New Sunset Western Garden Book*, 9th ed. Birmingham, AL: Oxmoor House.

Brickell, Christopher. 2004. *American Horticultural Society A to Z Encyclopedia of Garden Plants*, rev. U.S. ed. New York: DK Publishing.

Brookes, John. 1991. *The Book of Garden Design*. New York: Wiley.

Chalker-Scott, Linda. 2008. *The Informed Gardener*. Seattle: University of Washington Press.

———. *The Informed Gardener Blooms Again*. Seattle: University of Washington Press.

Chatto, Beth. 2000. *Beth Chatto's Gravel Garden*. London: Frances Lincoln.

———. 2005. *Beth Chatto's Woodland Garden*. London: Cassell Illustrated.

———. 2006. *Beth Chatto's Damp Garden*, rev. ed. London: Cassell Illustrated.

Darke, Rick. 2007. *The Encyclopedia of Grasses for Livable Landscapes*. Portland, OR: Timber Press.

Deardorff, David, and Kathryn Wadsworth. 2009. *What's Wrong with My Plant? (And How Do I Fix It?): A Visual Guide to Easy Diagnosis and Organic Remedies*. Portland, OR: Timber Press.

Dirr, Michael A. 2011. *Dirr's Encyclopedia of Trees and Shrubs*. Portland, OR: Timber Press.

DiSabato-Aust, Tracy. 2003. *The Well-Tended Perennial Garden: Planting and Pruning Techniques*. Portland, OR: Timber Press.

Halpin, Anne (ed.). 2001. *Sunset Northeastern Garden Book*. Menlo Park, CA: Sunset Publishing Corporation.

Hogan, Sean. 2008. *Trees for All Seasons: Broadleaved Evergreens for Temperate Climates*. Portland, OR: Timber Press.

Kelly, John (ed.). 2004. *Hilliers: The Gardener's Guide to Trees and Shrubs*. Newton Abbot, UK: David and Charles.

Lancaster, Roy. 1995. *What Plant Where*. New York: Dorling Kindersley.

Lawson, Andrew. 1996. *The Gardener's Book of Color*. London: Frances Lincoln.

Lloyd, Christopher. 2001. *The Well-Tempered Garden*, rev. ed. London: Cassell and Co.

———. 2004. *Christopher Lloyd's Gardening Year*. London: Frances Lincoln.

———. 2005. *Succession Planting for Year-round Pleasure*. Portland, OR: Timber Press.

Lord, Tony, and Andrew Lawson. 2008. *Encyclopedia of Planting Combinations*. Buffalo, NY: Firefly Books.

Lovejoy, Ann. 2001. *Ann Lovejoy's Organic Garden Design School*. Emmaus, PA: Rodale.

Ogden, Lauren Springer. 2011. *The Undaunted Garden: Planting for Weather-Resilient Beauty*, 2nd ed. Golden, CO: Fulcrum Publishing.

Ogden, Lauren Springer, and Scott Ogden. 2011. *Water-

wise Plants for Sustainable Gardens: 200 Beautiful Drought-Tolerant Choices for All Climates. Portland, OR: Timber Press.

Pavord, Anna. 2009. *Bulb*. London: Mitchell Beazley.

———. 2010. *The Curious Gardener: A Year in the Garden*. London: Bloomsbury.

Rice, Graham. 2011. *Planting the Dry Shade Garden: The Best Plants for the Toughest Spot in Your Garden*. Portland, OR: Timber Press.

Schenk, George. 2002. *The Complete Shade Gardener*. Portland, OR: Timber Press.

———. 2003. *Gardening on Pavement, Tables, and Hard Surfaces*. Portland, OR: Timber Press.

Thomas, Graham Stuart. 1984. *The Art of Planting*. Boston, MA: David R. Godine.

———. 1990. *Perennial Garden Plants: Or the Modern Florilegium*. London: J. M. Dent & Sons.

———. 1992. *Ornamental Shrubs, Climbers and Bamboos*. Portland, OR: Sagapress / Timber Press.

———. 2002. *The Garden Through the Year*. Sagaponack, NY: Sagapress.

Toogood, Alan (ed.). 2003. *The Royal Horticultural Society, Propagating Plants*, 2nd ed. London: Dorling Kindersley.

Turnbull, Cass, and Kate Allen. 2004. *Cass Turnbull's Guide to Pruning: What, When, Where, and How to Prune for a More Beautiful Garden*. Seattle, WA: Sasquatch Books.

METRIC CONVERSIONS

INCHES	CENTIMETERS
$1/4$	0.6
$1/3$	0.8
$1/2$	1.25
1	2.5
2	5.0
3	7.5
4	10
5	12.5
6	15
7	18
8	20
9	23
10	25

FEET	METERS
$1/4$	0.08
$1/3$	0.1
$1/2$	0.15
1	0.3
2	0.6
3	0.9
4	1.2
5	1.5
6	1.8
7	2.1
8	2.4
9	2.7
10	3.0

U.S. GALLONS	LITRES
$1/2$	1.89
1	3.79
2	7.57
5	18.93
10	37.85

TEMPERATURES

$$°C = 5/9 × (°F - 32)$$
$$°F = (9/5 × °C) + 32$$

Index